ELECTRIC EATS

Recipes & Techniques To Make the Most of Your Kitchen Appliances

see the possibilities

ELECTRIC EATS

Recipes & Techniques To Make the Most of Your Kitchen Appliances

Alison DuBois Scutte

PUBLISHED BY:

Powerline Publishing Group
Delray Beach, Florida

Line Illustrations by Merritt Horan
Photography by Wes Pratt
Foodstyling by Patrick McGannon
Creative Direction by Alison Scutte
Cover and Content design by www.platinumgraphicsinc.com

Manufactured in the United States of America

Acknowledgements

For his never-ending love, support and patience with me, the kids and our ever-evolving household, I say thank you, thank you, thank you to my wonderful husband Al

I would also like to thank our children Max, Merritt, Josie and Ryann for bringing supreme joy and laughter to my life.

I am also very grateful to the wonderful kitchen staff at HSN (Fric, Carol and Carmelita) and my own Bravetti crew (Todd, Doug, Frank, Al and Al III) for all the hard work and dedication that goes into making my demonstrations successful…I couldn't do it without you guys! Thanks also to Zack Gross and Tracy Krause for their awesome Foodstyling that makes my on-air food look so yummy!

Finally, I would like to thank the great folks at Euro-Pro/Bravetti (Mark, Stanley, Aviva, Max and Sarah) for giving me the continued opportunity to work for their company!

Table of Contents

Foreword

I want to thank my many friends who watch me on The Home Shopping Network and for making my first book, Home Style Flavor with Flair, a great success! I received many complements from you on my home-style recipes however, many of you felt that the recipes took too much time for your busy schedules.

This book is dedicated to those of you who want to make great homey meals, but you want to make them quickly! I hope that you find my brand new recipes, as well as quicker versions of some of my recipes that appeared in Home Style Flavor with Flair, delicious as well as easy to make.

I hear from you occasionally, either through testimonial calls during one of my live presentations or in direct emails to me and I am pleased that so many of you report that you absolutely love the appliances that you have purchased after watching one of my demonstrations on HSN!

It has been called to my attention, however, that when you get the products home, you aren't quite certain how to use them properly. I am hearing that the instruction booklets that come with the product give you the basic information but do not give you all the little tips that make using the products completely effective and fun to use.

I am writing this book, and including the recipes I use on HSN, In hopes of answering your questions about the appliances you have purchased. However, these tips and recipes will work with virtually any brand appliance you own, no matter where you purchased it!

Part I of the book is packed with tips that will help you enjoy, and be successful using, your appliances As you try out the recipes included in Part II of this book, please refer back to the tips on the specific appliance that you are using and I think you will find that you will get the results you desire. However, these tips are my personal opinions and things I have learned. They should not replace any instructions or warnings that came from the manufacture with the product.

Good Luck and Happy Cooking,

PART II

TIPS & TECHNIQUES FOR USING YOUR APPLIANCES

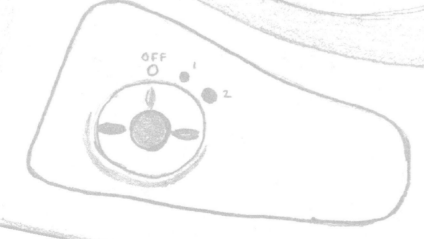

USING YOUR
FOOD PROCESSOR

Using Your Food Processor!

FOOD PROCESSOR

No matter what brand Food Processor you own, there are tricks to making it work for you! Traditionally, Food Processors have two blades for chopping. However, Bravetti, the appliance manufacturer I represent on HSN, has reinvented the food processor with its introduction of the quad-blade system. Using four blades is infinitely better than the two blade processors of the past because the end results of chopping will be uniform instead of a mixture of puree, mincing and chopping.

Currently there are three models of Bravetti food processors available that utilize the quad blade system; The Quad Blade Processor, The Maxi Chopper and The Quad Blade Food Prep Center. If you do not own one of the quad blade systems, I encourage you to purchase one—you will not be sorry. There are also various accessories that came with, or are available, to complement your Food Processor. Please refer to the Using Your Accessories guide at the end of this section for additional information that will enable you to perform many kitchen tasks.

Although the recipes in this book that utilize a food processor give specific directions, there are several basic things for you to know to get the best results from your processor. There is a Quick Guide to a Perfect Chop at the end of this section, but please take the time to read the General Information on Chopping below; I think you will be glad you did!

Using Your Food Processor!

GENERAL INFORMATION ON CHOPPING

Whether you are using one of the Food Processors or the Maxi Chopper, there are capacity markings on your food processor bowl; 6 cups or 7 cups respectively. Never go above the markings (even though there is additional room) because 1) the end results will not be good and 2) it is messy if you have a spill over when the blades start swirling the food around! In fact, I hardly ever fill the bowl beyond 5 cups.

However, the term "5 cups" can be misleading. It is easy to measure and process 5 cups of canned tomatoes but what does 5 cups translate into in regards to fresh tomatoes? What about harder, tougher foods like meats, onions or fresh carrots?

It really doesn't matter the exact food you are chopping, what is really important is 1) the food hardness, 2) the texture 3) the amount of liquid in the food and 3) the size. To get a good end result, you must give the blades room to chop the foods properly. For example, if you are chopping onion you will get much better results if you do 2-3 at a time rather than to pack the machine too tightly. So use your best judgment when loading the processor bowl to give the food ample room to be chopped; it is always better to do 2 perfectly chopped batches than 1 uneven batch.

When using your processor to prepare recipes not listed in this book, you should know that the quantity of whole foods you put into the bowl is not necessarily how much you will end up with once the food is chopped. For example, 6 cups of whole mushrooms will come down to about 4 cups coarsely chopped or 2 cups finely chopped! After you use the processor a few times you will get the hang of "eyeballing" vegetables at the produce stand and know what will yield 1 cup. To get you started, I have found that 1 medium onion, 2 medium tomatoes or 1/4 of a small cabbage all equal about 1 cup when chopped!

Using Your Food Processor!

Preparing fresh foods to go into the processor bowl is very similar to preparing them to chop with a knife; only you don't have to do the actual chopping! Always wash and pat dry your foods and if you would normally remove the peeling, seeds, roots or stems, then do so. Cut the food into reasonable-sized pieces of no more than a 2 1/2 inch cube, a 4" length or a 4" sphere.

When loading the processor bowl, insert the blades first and then put in the food. As discussed above, do not crowd the blades with hard whole foods! Try to place the foods from the bottom upwards evenly disbursing the load. For example, do not lay a half of an onion across the top of the blades. Instead, slide it lengthwise down the side; be careful not to cut yourself on the blades! If you are chopping celery, carrots or anything that is in stalks, place them vertical in the bowl instead of lying down. If you are chopping meat, raw or cooked, do not load the bowl first, turn the machine on a medium high speed first and then drop the pieces into the food shoot. Otherwise you may end up with Pate!

Using Your Food Processor!

If you are making something that requires multiple ingredients, try to layer them using the following tips:

- Liquid should go in last so that it covers the food in the bowl before it settles to the bottom.
- Fresh herbs with stems should be placed between ingredients whereas dry spices can go on the top.
- The hardest items should be near the bottom.
- Soft cheeses should go toward the bottom.

For example, if you were making a salsa you first put in the onion, then the cilantro followed by the peppers and tomatoes. Top with your dry seasonings and cover all with the lemon or tomato juice.

Another example, spinach artichoke dip, would start with the cream cheese and be followed by the artichokes, spinach, lemon and seasonings!

Speed determines the size of the chop and the texture of the end result. I always start by quickly pressing the pulse button 2-3 times and then checking the chop; it is usually perfect. If a few pieces are too large, do not continue processing to get them chopped as you will over-chop the rest. Just remove the under chopped pieces and pulse them again separately after the rest has been removed.

The only time I find it necessary to turn the processor on a medium to high speed is if I am 1) chopping something extremely hard like ice or frozen fruit, 2) making a puree or creamed soup, 3) making a layered dip that uses cream cheese or canned beans/peas or 4) grinding meat. But, even with these items, I pulse a few times first before turning the machine onto a moderate speed until desired consistency is reached.

The worst thing you can do is to over-process something. Remember you can always process more if something is too chunky but you can't reverse the process if it's too mushy!

Using Your Food Processor!

FOOD PROCESSOR

Fresh fruits and vegetables:

- Remove any coarse, thick, papery or undesirable peels from foods such as onions, garlic, citrus fruits and melons.
- Cut off and discard the root and/or stem.
- Cut away any bruised, brown or hard spots.
- Cut all onions and large tomatoes in half (lengthwise).
- Celery, broccoli, zucchini and the likes should be cut into pieces no longer than 4 inches.
- Load the veggies into the machine from the bottom up evenly disbursing the load.
- Place long items in vertically, not horizontally.
- If layering veggies or fruits, place the harder ones near the bottom and softer ones on top.
- Do not crowd the blades!
- Always use the pulse button to avoid over-processing.

Raw meats:

- Trim away any large areas of fat.
- Wash the meat and pat dry.
- Cut the meat into strips, against the grain if possible, no larger than 2 1/2" wide X 2 1/2" thick X 4" long.
- Turn the machine on a medium-high speed and drop the meat, one piece at a time, down the food shoot and process until the desired texture is reached.
- If making a meatloaf, meatballs, etc. pulse the veggies first then turn on the machine and drop the mea through the food shoot.
- If adding seasoning to raw meat, add it immediately after the last piece of meat has been dropped through the food shoot so the spices get mixed in but the meat is not over processed.

Cooked Meats:

- Trim away any large areas of fat.
- Cut the meat into strips, against the grain if possible, no larger than 2 1/2" wide X 2 1/2" thick X 4" long.
- Load the meat into the processor bowl and pulse until desired texture is reached.
- If making a meat salad, pulse the onions and/or celery 2 times first, then place meat, seasonings and mayonnaise into processor and process at low speed until desired texture is reached.

FOOD PROCESSOR

Using Your Food Processor!

Dough Blade:

Use your dough blade to make bread dough, pizza dough, pie crusts, cookie dough, biscuits and anything else that is thick and needs to be mixed and/or kneaded.

When using the dough blade, insert the blade and add all dry ingredients. Turn the machine on a medium speed and add the butter, oil, water or other liquid slowly down the food shoot. Adjust your speed as necessary to accommodate the amount and thickness of the ingredients you are mixing. You can easily make a 2 lb. bread mix or 2 pizzas crusts at one time.

I often use my dough blade after I have chopped or shredded something into the bowl. I simply remove the other blade, insert the dough blade and dry ingredients and continue as directed above! You can make great cheese biscuits, olive breads, onion rolls, etc. by using multiple blades.

The dough blade is also great for recipes calling for soft cheeses; cheese dips, cheese cakes, ricotta mixtures and holiday cheese balls. Canned meat salads and spreads like tuna, chicken, beef, or ham can also be made using the dough blade as well as crab and fish cakes.

Basically, if you want to mix something very well, but not chop it, reach for your dough blade. As with chopping, start on a low speed and increase as necessary to achieve the desired results.

Slicing, Shredding, Grating & French Fry Blades:

There are various blades that came with your Processor to accomplish many food prep tasks. The product manual gave instructions on how to insert the blades for use, but there are a couple of tips that will help you enjoy using the blades more.

First, selection and preparing the veggies are important. Try to use firm, straight vegetables as close to the size of the food shoot as possible. Then cut off both ends so that it will fit flat next to the blade and the pusher.

Using Your Food Processor!

FOOD PROCESSOR

Next, position the food securely into the food shoot. If you are working with carrots, celery or other thin vegetables, you may want to put 2-3 in the shoot at the same time; this way the veggie will be secured in an upright position and not end up being pulled sideways across the blade!

After, the veggies are loaded, turn the machine to the lowest speed and apply gentle, even pressure to push the veggies down. Adjust your speed as necessary to the hardness of the vegetable. Potatoes and carrots will require a higher speed than tomatoes or cucumbers.

Whipping Attachment:

The whipping attachment is great for whipped cream and meringue. Place the blade in first and then add the liquid. I never whip more than 3 cups of cream or 8 egg whites (room temperature) at a time. Turn the machine to the highest speed for 30 seconds or so, slow it down to low speed and add sugar or spices slowly through the food shoot and then continue on high until done. Watch it; it whips very fast! When you see the level of cream pulling down, check the texture. If you go to long, you will make butter—which is OK but refer to the butter recipe in this book for the particulars!

Whisk Attachment:

Use your whisk attachment as you would a hand mixer. The only trick is to add the liquid first so the cake mix or other dry ingredients don't get stuck to the bottom. After the ingredients are in the bowl, put in the whisk and turn on the machine to a medium speed. You will probably have to stop and scrape down the sides of the bowl and then continue mixing until the batter is smooth. Try using the chopping blades first to chop a little onion, pepper and ham. Then add 3 eggs and some water. Put in the whisk attachment and turn it to a medium speed—you are now ready to make your western omelet!

Other Attachments:

The other attachments you received are pretty self-explanatory so I will not go into detail about them! I hope this information has been enlightening and will help you get the most from your Bravetti Food Processor. If you have further questions, please email me at the address listed in the Introduction and I will help you all I can!

USING YOUR
FLASH FRYER

Tips to Perfect Flash Frying

FLASH FRYER

Bravetti introduced the concept of Flash Frying to North America and was the first to bring it to HSN! Now, many manufacturers offer Flash Fryers. Those of you who have purchased a Flash Fryer are already appreciating the difference between Flash Frying and traditional frying in a pan or deep fryer with out the Flash Frying technology.

True Flash Fryers have the heating element and the thermostat submerged directly in the oil. This controls the heat of the oil so that a consistent temperature is maintained while adding fresh or frozen food. Without heat fluctuation, your foods turn out light, crispy and virtually oil free; the whole point of flash frying!

There are just a few tips you should know when using your fryer. Whether you have a 3 liter, a 5 liter, digital or not, cool-touch or stainless these tips will work for you!

- I use pure Vegetable Oil when frying, but you can use Canola, Peanut or a Blend. Never use Olive Oil; it will smoke!

- Try to buy the oil in bottles that have a large opening at the top (I shop at the wholesale stores for this) and keep the oil container for later!

- Never fill the Reservoir above the Maximum or below the Minimum Fill Lines! Those lines are there as a safety net against boil-over or smoking. Please follow this rule!

- Make sure the fryer is properly preheated! Depending on the size of your fryer, this can take between 8 – 10 minutes.

- Do not crowd the food! It will cook faster and more even if there is room for the oil to circulate around the food.

- Even though the instructions say to put the food into the basket and then lower it, you will have problems doing this if you are using batter; it will stick! Lower the basket first and then use long tongs and gently lower the item into the basket. If you do not feel comfortable doing this, dip the basket into the oil to coat it first and then immediately place the food into it; it will help but not alleviate the problem.

FLASH FRYER

Tips to Perfect Flash Frying

- Speaking of batter, make sure the batter is thick enough to cling tightly to the food. If using tempura or beer batter, this is especially important. Otherwise little pieces will float to the top and burn after awhile. If this happens, try to get them out with a slotted spoon or sieve before they burn and taint the flavor of the oil!

- The temperature guide is great but, personally, I fry everything on the highest temperature. The exceptions are large frozen egg rolls and anything battered in bread crumbs; I drop the temperature of 10 degrees for those two things!

- If you are going to make fresh French Fries or other vegetables that are not breaded, take care to dry them thoroughly with paper towels before you put them in the fryer! I cannot over emphasize the importance of this! If you do not, your oil could boil over and be dangerous or at the very least extremely messy.

- If you are frying steak or other red meat, bread first and then carefully place into the oil one piece at a time and then cover immediately with the lid. I find that red meats "pop" so I always try to use the lid as quickly as possible.

- If you are making Funnel Cakes or Rosettes, remove the basket completely. You will need a wire spoon to remove the cake, but otherwise they will stick to the basket and be rectangle in shape!

- Cooking times will vary depending on 1) quantity cooking, 2) temperature of the food and 3) size of the food. But generally speaking foods are typically done when the outside reaches a medium to dark golden brown color. However, I always recommend removing one item and test for doneness before removing the entire batch. Below are some of the foods you may fry and the time it normally takes me to cook one basket, half-full.

  * Bread-like foods such as doughnuts, French toast sticks, Hush Puppies and Fritters will usually float when they are done, but to be safe, remove one and test for doneness.

  * Frozen munchie-type foods are typically done when the outside reaches a medium to dark golden brown color; small things like Cheese Sticks, Poppers and Pizza Rolls are done in about 3-4 minutes!

  * Frozen Shrimp are done in about 5-6 minutes.

Tips to Perfect Flash Frying

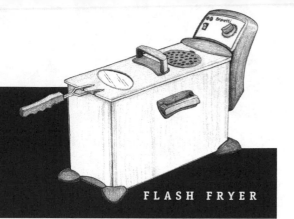

FLASH FRYER

* Large pieces of chicken (bone-in) usually take me 8-10 minutes to cook depending on the amount chicken you are cooking at one time.

* Fish filets, depending on thickness, typically take 4-6 minutes to cook.

* Fresh French fries require about 8-8 minutes to thoroughly cook and be crispy.

* Larger frozen foods like Egg-Rolls and Corn Dogs, will take about 5 minutes.

• After you are finished frying, unplug the unit and remove the lid. Allow the oil to completely cool; this could take 2 hours or more but don't rush this step. Then, what I do is place the original oil container into the sink and cover the mouth with cheese cloth or a small mesh sieve. Carefully pour the oil through the mesh into the container. If I was frying chicken or steak, I stop before I get to the "sledge" at bottom of the reservoir! Then seal the container and store the oil in the refrigerator. If you didn't keep the oil container or don't want to use it, strain the oil in the fryer into a large bowl and store in that or wash the reservoir, replace the oil, cover tightly and store in the refrigerator!

CAUTION

Be sure and check the manufacturer's food capacity limit in your owner's manual. Never exceed the limits!

Those of you who watch HSN see me fry a whole cut-up chicken in the 5 liter fryer. I never filled the oil beyond the fill-line and am very careful to add one piece at a time to make sure the weight of the chicken does not push the oil up too high and boil over. I do that demonstration at my own risk and do not recommend you doing it at home!

USING YOUR
CONVECTION & ROTISSERIE OVEN

Using Your Convection & Rotisserie Oven!

ROTISSERIE OVEN

I love my Convection Rotisserie Oven not just because it is faster, but because it is handier than my large oven and I don't have to wait so long to pre-heat!

Convection cooking uses a fan to circulate the hot air around the food thus cooking it about 25% faster than traditional ovens. It also produces foods that are golden brown outside while remaining juicy and tender on the inside; perfect! I love cooking with convection and I think you will too!

Many manufacturers sell convection ovens, rotisserie ovens and combination convection with rotisserie ovens.   Although the capacity and the rotisserie feature may vary, the basic techniques do not. Below are some basic things you should know about Convection cooking in General, Convection Roasting, Convection Broiling & Using your Rotisserie.

CONVECTION COOKING IN GENERAL

- The oven uses a large amount of electrical wattage to work properly. Make sure that it is plugged into a wall outlet all by itself. If an appliance like a coffee maker or toaster (even if it is not turned on at the time) shares the receptacle, electrical current will be drawn away from the oven causing it not to reach optimal temperatures.

- Preheating; necessary or not? I have cooked with and without preheating the oven and the difference is the time it takes to cook the food once it is in the oven. If the oven is already hot, the food cooks faster; not exactly rocket science to figure that out! So, what I do is turn the oven on when I start preparing the food to go in and however long it takes me to prepare the food is how long I preheat! If I am cooking dinner rolls, I haven't preheated as long as I did if I was making a cake, but it seems to work!

- When cooking in your convection oven it is necessary to reduce the temperature recommended in recipes and on the package of frozen foods by 25°F. You will find that I will list temperatures for both conventional and convection ovens in my recipes to avoid any confusion!

Using Your Convection & Rotisserie Oven!

- Because the cooking time is up to 25% quicker in your convection oven, be sure to check your food earlier than normal. I reduce the time called for in the recipe by 25%, set my timer and then check the food in 3 minute intervals until it is done to my liking. I did not include convection cooking times in my recipes as different models will have varying cooking times so be sure to adjust your timing as directed above! Refer to the cooking time chart included in your Owner's Manual for average cooking times.

- One rack or two? Because of the fan circulating the air, you can bake on either one or two racks. However, the type of pan you choose and food placement is important; you want to give room for the air to circulate properly. For example, if you are baking two cake pans at once, stagger them so one pan is back further and one is toward the front. If baking two layer cakes, put them on the same rack but allow 4-5 inches between them. I do not recommend baking two cookie sheets at once, unless you alternate racks halfway into the cooking time, because the air flow is blocked and the bottom will cook faster than the top.

- If you are baking on two racks it may take a little longer to reach the desired doneness than if cooking on one rack.

- Any cookware/ bake ware that is oven-safe for a conventional oven, will work in your convection oven. This includes heat-resistant paper and plastic containers that manufactures recommend for use in conventional ovens. However,

  * Shallow pans with lower sides allow the air to circulate and work the best.

  * Avoid using pans that are so large they cover the entire rack.

  * Dark or matte finish bake ware will produce darker browning on food surfaces.

  * Aluminum foil reflects the heat away from food and increases the cooking time.

  * Aluminum or silver-colored bake ware produces the fastest results.

Using Your Convection & Rotisserie Oven!

ROTISSERIE OVEN

CONVECTION ROASTING

- When roasting meats, it is not necessary to preheat.

- Cooking times will be between 25-30% quicker, so adjust your timing and check periodically with a meat thermometer to obtain desired results. Refer to the cooking time chart in your Owner's Manual for average cooking times.

- Roast meats and poultry in a shallow pan with low sides for best results. However, add about 1/4 inch of water to the pan to avoid splattering oils. Add water as necessary throughout the cooking process.

- When seasoning the meats, the redder the spice, the darker brown the outside of the meat will be. For example, paprika on a chicken can make the skin burn; cover the meat with foil if the outside is getting too dark.

- If basting meats with Bar-B-Q Sauce, Honey, Preserves or anything that contains a lot of sugar, apply the sauce, by brush, only in the last 10-15 minutes to prevent burning.

CONVECTION BROILING

- Always use the broiling pan that came with your oven. It is designed to minimize smoking and splattering!

- Position the rack in the center of the oven for cut of meat 1î or less and on the bottom rack for meats over 1î in thickness. Move the rack to the very top for the last 1 minute of cooking if a darker brown color or heavier crispness is desired.

- Slice or slit fat evenly around the outside edges of steaks and chops to prevent curling.

- Use tongs when turning meat to prevent piercing the meat and loosing juices.

- If desired, marinate meats or chicken before broiling. Brush on additional marinade or sauce only in the last 5 minutes of cooking to prevent burning.

ROTISSERIE OVEN

Using Your Convection & Rotisserie Oven!

USING YOUR ROTISSERIE

The Rotisserie feature and included accessory items in your oven varies greatly depending on the model of oven you purchased. Please refer to your Owner's Manual for size limits and skewer assembly instructions. Below are some basic tips that are pertinent to all models.

- Trim large cuts of beef or pork to remove any fat from the outside edge.

- When putting the meat onto the spit rod keep it centered and balanced. Otherwise, the food may actually fall off or hit the heating element causing the machine to stop or stall or the food to catch fire!

- When placing the food on the spit rod, remember that the end is sharp so take care not to push toward your hand!

- After the meat is on the spit, season as desired. When seasoning the meats, the redder the spice, the darker brown the outside of the meat will be. For example, paprika on a chicken can make the skin burn; cover the meat with foil if the outside is getting too dark. Also, if basting meats with Bar-B-Que Sauce, Honey, Preserves or anything that contains a lot of sugar, apply the sauce, by brush, only in the last 10-15 minutes to prevent burning. There are several recipes for rotisserie seasoning rubs in this book. Check the index for page numbers.

- Some meats and chickens should be tied. It is easier to do this once the meat is on the spit rod. Use cotton kitchen string to tie the chicken's legs and wings to prevent flopping around during cooking or to truss a beef roast tightly together. Wetting the ends of the string before tying will keep it from burning.

- If the oven makes a groaning noise while the rotisserie is activated, lubricate the gear wheel with a Q-Tip and a drop or two of vegetable oil.

Using Your Convection & Rotisserie Oven!

ROTISSERIE OVEN

- To remove the meat from the oven, turn the rotisserie off first and then use the handle that came with the unit. Lift first from the side that is not inserted into the oven wall and then gentle release the other side.

- To test the met for doneness, remove the roast and use a meat thermometer in the thickest part of the meat; just be careful not to hit the spit rod in the meat!

- When the meat is done, place it on a cutting board or platter and allow it to rest for 5-10 minutes. Removing the spit rod or cutting the meat too early will release the juices and the meat will rapidly become dry.

- Use a kitchen towel or triple thick paper towels to prevent your fingers from burning when removing the spit rod.

- Tips for using the Rotisserie Basket (not included with all models) :

  * Make sure the basket is closed tightly to keep the food from shifting during cooking.

  * You want the food to be secure, but not packed together. Try to leave a little room between the items so that all sides will cook evenly. If you are cooking a small number of things, crumple aluminum foil and stuff into the corners to prevent food from sliding around.

  * Coat the basket with non-stick spray before loading to prevent the food from sticking.

  * Make sure no food is sticking out of the oven to prevent it from hitting the element.

  * Try cooking steaks, burgers, peppers or anything else you would normally grill. You will get great results without the hassles of grilling!

PART II
RECITES FOR YOUR KITCHEN APPLIANCES

GOOD MORNING!
BREAKFAST & BRUNCH

FOOD PROCESSOR

Homemade Breakfast Sausage Patties

Makes 8 Patties

1 lb. Boneless Pork Loins

1/4 teaspoon rubbed sage

1/4 teaspoon marjoram

1/4 teaspoon coriander

1/4 teaspoon fennel seeds

1 teaspoon salt

1/2 teaspoon ground black pepper

Try this delicious, lower-fat version of traditional store-bought breakfast sausage! Try serving them sandwiched between Southern-Style Biscuits with the cheese option; heavenly!

PREPARATION:

Wash and pat dry the pork loins. Cut the loins in half lengthwise.

Mix all spices together into a small bowl.

Install the chopping blades inside your Bravetti Quad-Blade Food Processor; attach lid. Turn the processor on and set to speed 9. Drop the loin strips, on at a time, through the feed shoot and process until smooth. Add the seasonings and continue processing on a medium speed until well blended.

Form into 8 patties and fry in pan over medium heat.

VARIATION:

Increase the coriander to 1/2 teaspoon for a hotter version!

2

Southern-Style Cheese Biscuits

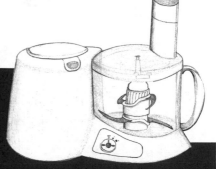

FOOD PROCESSOR

Traditional biscuits of the South use Buttermilk to make them light and fluffy. If you do not have buttermilk, use the variation recipe at the bottom of the page.

PREPARATION:

Using the thin shredding blade attached to your Food Processor, shred the cheese, then remove the shredding blade and insert the dough blade and proceed as directed below.

Using the dough blade attachment in your food processor, add all ingredients, except the buttermilk, and process lightly using your pulse button. When ingredients are mixed well, turn processor onto lowest speed and pour buttermilk slowly into the food shoot, adjusting the speed faster as needed.

Remove dough and place onto a lightly floured board. Roll it out to about a 1/2 inch thickness. Cut the dough with a biscuit, or round cookie, cutter and place onto a well-greased pan.

Bake for 15 minutes in a 425° pre-heated oven.

VARIATION:

If you do not have buttermilk, use the following ingredients instead and follow the directions above!

2 cups all-purpose flour
1/2 teaspoon salt
2 teaspoons sugar
4 teaspoons baking powder
1/2 teaspoon cream of tartar
1/2 cup shortening
2/3 cup milk

INGREDIENTS

2 cups all-purpose flour

3/4 tsp salt

3 teaspoons baking powder

1 teaspoon baking soda

4 tablespoons shortening

1 cup buttermilk (if not using, follow variation recipe below)

6 oz. sharp cheddar cheese

Zucchini & Carrot Nut Muffins

INGREDIENTS

Makes 12 Muffins

1 medium zucchini; ends trimmed

1 medium carrot; peeled & ends trimmed

1 large egg

1/2 cup vegetable oil

1 cups sugar

1 teaspoon vanilla

1 1/2 cups flour

1/2 teaspoon salt

1/2 teaspoon baking powder

1/2 teaspoon baking soda

1 teaspoon cinnamon

1/4 teaspoon nutmeg

1/2 cup walnuts

These moist muffins will soon be a family favorite!
This recipe can be made very quickly in your Food Processor.

PREPARATION:

Cut the zucchini and carrot into thirds and place into your Quad-Blade Food Processor; pulse several times until the mixture is well chopped. Add the remaining ingredients, in order listed, and process on low speed until well mixed.

Grease a 12-muffin tin or spray with non-stick spray. Fill each cup 2/3 with batter.

Preheat Conventional Oven to 400° or Convection Oven to 375°.

Bake for 13 to 16 minutes or until done.

IF YOU DO NOT HAVE A FOOD PROCESSOR:

Shred the zucchini and carrots. Chop the nuts.

In a large bowl, beat the egg until light and frothy. Mix in the oil and sugar.

Stir in the carrots, zucchini and vanilla. Combine the flour and remaining ingredients and stir into the egg mixture.

Bake as directed above.

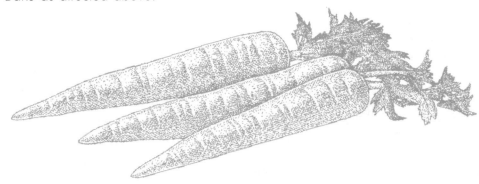

4

Apple Cinnamon Loaf Bread

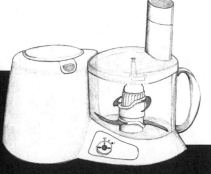

FOOD PROCESSOR

This is delicious any time of day! Try spreading cinnamon butter over a hot slice!

PREPARATION:

Preheat Conventional oven to 350° or Convection Oven to 325°.

Peel, core and thinly slice the apples; place them in bowl of cool water with 1 tablespoon Lemon juice.

Combine the remaining ingredients using the dough blade in your Quad-Blade Food Processor or a hand mixer.

Pour batter into a well greased 9x5 inch loaf pan.

Drain the apple slices and place them on top of the batter.

Bake in the center of the oven 55 to 60 minutes or until inserted toothpick comes out fairly clean. Remove from oven and let cool 10 minutes. Remove from pan and cool on wire rack or serve warm!

QUICKER VERSION:

Make this recipe into muffins and bake at 400° Conventional or 375° Convection for 15 to 14 minutes!

IF YOU DO NOT HAVE A FOOD PROCESSOR:

Shred the apples. In a large bowl, beat the egg, butter and sugar until smooth. Stir in the apples. Combine the flour and remaining ingredients and stir into the egg mixture.

Bake as directed above.

INGREDIENTS

3 medium granny smith apples; about 3 cup peeled, cored & sliced.

1 tablespoon Lemon juice

1 stick butter; softened and cut into thirds

2 large eggs

1 cup sugar

2 cups all-purpose flour

1 teaspoon baking powder

1/2 teaspoon baking soda

1/2 teaspoon salt

1 teaspoon cinnamon

1 teaspoon vanilla extract

Breakfast Sausage Casserole

INGREDIENTS

1 pound ground pork sausage (homemade or store bought)

1 tablespoon butter

1 small onion; finely chopped (optional)

8 slices white bread; toasted and cut into cubes

2 cups sharp cheddar cheese; shredded

8 eggs; beaten

3 cups milk

1/2 teaspoon salt

1/4 teaspoon coarse ground pepper

This is a great make-ahead dish to serve when friends and family are staying at your house and you want to cut down on morning mayhem!

PREPARATION:

Make the sausage using your food processor according to directions in Breakfast Sausage Patties Recipe; or use store bought.

Crumble the sausage in a medium, non-stick skillet and cook over medium heat until evenly browned; drain.

Wipe out the skillet and return to the stove. Add the butter and the onions and brown over medium-low heat until onions are soft and beginning to brown; remove from heat and set aside.

Use the dough blade of your food processor, and beat the eggs and the milk on low speed, until well combined. Add the sausage, onion, cheese, salt and pepper and pulse once or twice.

Place the bread cubes even across the bottom of a greased 9x13x2 inch baking dish. Pour mixture over all.

Cover and refrigerate 8 hours or overnight.

Preheat Oven to 350°.

Bake, covered, for 50 minutes. Uncover and bake another 30 minutes or until the casserole has risen, the center is set and a golden brown color is achieved.

Remove from oven and allow to cool 5-10 minutes before slicing. Serve as is or with salsa.

Cheesy Grits & Bacon Bake

Making an entire breakfast, including grits, requires many pots and perfect timing. I developed this recipe as a way to get everything I like for breakfast – but in one dish! Now, when it's ready, all I have to make is the toast! Try it and see what you think!

PREPARATION:

Pre-heat your Conventional Oven to 350° or your Convection Oven to 325°. Grease or coat with non-stick spray an 8x10 baking dish.

In a 3 quart (or larger) saucepan, stir the grits into cold water. Place over medium heat and cook, stirring often, for 5 minutes. Add the milk and butter and continue cooking another 10 minutes, stirring frequently. The grits will just come to a low boil at the end of cooking, but will be thick. Remove from heat.

Quickly stir in the beaten eggs, cheese and salt.

Pour 1/2 the mixture into the baking dish. Sprinkle the crumbled bacon evenly on mixture and top with the remaining grit mixture.

Bake, uncovered, for 30 minutes.

VARIATIONS:

Variation 1: Make as is but top with thinly sliced tomatoes and bake.

Variation 2: Substitute diced ham for the bacon and use Swiss instead of Cheddar.

INGREDIENTS

1 pound bacon; cooked, drained and crumbled

2 cups quick grits

4 cups water

2 cups milk

1 stick butter

8 ounces shredded sharp cheddar cheese

6 large eggs; beaten

1/2 teaspoon salt

Pepper to taste

Guava Stuffed French Toast

INGREDIENTS

1 small tin Guava paste

8 ounces cream cheese

1 loaf French bread

3 eggs

1/4 cup milk

Butter

Confectioner's sugar

This French Toast is incredibly good, but very rich! If you have never tried Guava, you are in for a real treat as it is excellent. Guava paste is usually found in the Latin/Ethnic section of your grocery store. If you cannot find Guava, you may use any flavor of All-Fruit Preserves that you like.

PREPARATION:

Remove the cream cheese from the refrigerator and let sit at room temperature for 10-15 minutes.

Slice the French bread into 2 – 2 1/2 inch thick slices. On the curved crust side, make a 1 inch slit with a thin serrated knife. Use your finger and gently slide it into the slit and push around enough to make a fair-sized pocket; careful not to tear through to the outside of the bread! Do this to each piece of bread.

Open the guava paste and place it onto a plate; repeat with the cream cheese. Slice the Guava and the cheese into thin strips; enough for each piece of bread to have at least one slice.

Gently push 1 slice of cream cheese, followed by 1 or more slices of Guava into each piece of bread. Stuff as much as you comfortably can into each piece without protruding through the opening.

Beat the eggs with the milk until frothy. Heat a large skillet over medium high and melt enough butter to just coat the bottom.

Dip the stuffed toast into the egg mixture and turn, lightly coating both sides; do not saturate the bread! Place the dipped bread, one slice at a time, into the hot pan of butter. Cook 1-2 minutes per side or until golden brown. Dust with powdered sugar and serve. Repeat until all the toast is cooked adding butter as necessary.

Easy Flash-Fryer Donut Bites

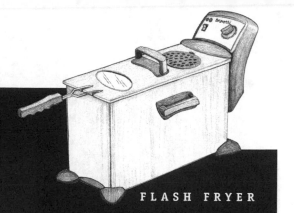

These are so fast and easy that I feel silly putting them into my cookbook! However, I get lots of emails on how to make them so here it is!

INGREDIENTS

1 can Pillsbury Orange Flavored Sweet Rolls

Vegetable Oil for Frying

PREPARATION:

Preheat fryer to 375°.

Pop open can and separate rolls, reserving icing for later. Cut each roll into quarters. Take each quarter wedge and stretch cut ends together to form a circle.

Using metal tongs, gently place the circles into lowered fry basket. Fry for about 4 minutes in covered fryer, turning after 3 minutes.

Raise basket and allow donuts to drain. Top with lightly warmed icing or powdered sugar.

HINT: I let my icing warm atop the fryer lid while frying!

NOTE:

You may be tempted to try using the Cinnamon Rolls instead of the Orange Flavored—don't! The cinnamon will burn and the oil in your fryer will be ruined!

Healthy Pancakes

INGREDIENTS

Makes 12 Pancakes

3/4 cup all-purpose flour

1/2 cup whole wheat flour

1/4 cup rolled oats

1/3 cup unsalted sunflower seeds

2 Tablespoons Wheat Germ

1 teaspoon baking powder

1/2 teaspoon baking soda

1/2 teaspoon cinnamon

1/4 teaspoon salt

1/2 cup low fat milk

1 cup plain low fat yogurt

1 large egg

2 Tablespoons honey

2 Tablespoons vegetable or canola oil

Healthy pancakes? Yes! Serve these tasty cakes without guilt–especially if you top with a little honey instead of syrup!

PREPARATION:

In a mixing bowl, mix together the dry ingredients. In a separate smaller bowl, beat the milk, yogurt, egg, honey and oil (using the lowest speed of your hand mixer) until well blended.

Heat griddle or non-stick skillet, over medium heat, until a drop of water will bounce and sputter. Spray pan with non-stick cooking spray. Spoon the batter onto the pan, spreading cakes to get the size you want; don't over-crowd.

When the entire cake is bubbly and the bubbles on the edge begin to break open (about 2 to 3 minutes), turn the cakes. Turn only once! The second side won't take as long so watch for it to be golden brown.

Serve with honey or maple syrup. Makes about 12 medium-small pancakes.

Blueberry Pancakes

These are the best with fresh blueberries but since fresh are not available year around, frozen will do. Either way, they sure beat plain 'ole pancakes!

PREPARATION:

Prepare the blueberries by washing, drying and picking off any stems. Discard any shriveled berries. If using frozen, place in a colander and run cold water over them until they are thawed. Pat dry and check to make sure no stem pieces remain.

In a mixing bowl, mix together the dry ingredients. Add the oil, milk and egg and blend together using the lowest speed of your hand mixer. When all of the large lumps are gone, use a wooden spoon and fold in the blueberries.

Heat griddle or non-stick skillet, over medium heat, until a drop of water will bounce and sputter. Spray pan with non-stick cooking spray. Spoon the batter onto the pan, spreading cakes to get the size you want; don't overcrowd.

When the entire cake is bubbly and the bubbles on the edge begin to break open (about 2 to 3 minutes), turn the cakes. Turn only once! The second side won't take as long so watch for it to be golden brown.

Serve with powdered sugar, maple syrup or Blueberry Sauce (see index for recipe location).

HINT: This recipe makes about 12 small pancakes so double it if you have a hungry crowd!

INGREDIENTS

Makes 12 Small Pancakes

1 cup flour

4 tablespoons sugar

2 teaspoons baking powder

1/2 teaspoon salt

3/4 cup milk

2 tablespoons vegetable oil

1 egg

1 1/2 - 2 cups fresh or frozen blueberries

Non-stick cooking spray

Mexi-Quiche

INGREDIENTS

1/4 pound lean ground beef

1 Tbsp. butter

1/4 cup onion; finely chopped

1 clove garlic; minced

1 10-ounce can Roteló tomatoes with chilies; drained

2 cups half 'n half

3 eggs

1/4 teaspoon salt

1/4 teaspoon cumin

1/4 teaspoon cayenne pepper

1/2 cup shredded Mexican Blend Cheese (Cheddar & Monterey Jack)

1 9" ready to bake piecrust

This quiche is really good any time of day! Even "real men" will eat this one!

PREPARATION:

Let the piecrust sit out of the refrigerator for 15 minutes to soften. Unfold and press into a 9" deep pie tin.

Fry the beef in a skillet until browned, rinse and drain in a colander. Add butter, onion and garlic to the skillet and cook gently about 3 minutes. Return the beef to the pan, add the Rotel and cook just until warm; remove from heat.

Pour half 'n half into a 4-6 cup glass measuring cup or bowl; microwave for 1 1/2 minutes. Remove from microwave and blend in the eggs, salt, cumin and cayenne pepper; use the balloon whisk attachment of your hand mixer or whisk by hand until eggs are completely incorporated into the half 'n half.

Sprinkle the beef mixture and the cheese evenly onto the bottom of the piecrust. Pour egg mixture over it.

Bake at 375° in a Conventional Oven or 350° in a Convection Oven for 35 to 40 minutes or until the top is golden brown. Slice and serve with salsa on the side.

Basic Waffles

This is a good basic recipe for light fluffy waffles. Using butter rather than oil will give you an extra richness and crunch!

PREPARATION:

Sift the dry ingredients together in a medium or large mixing bowl. In a smaller bowl, mix the milk, eggs and oil or butter together until the eggs are completely mixed.

Pour the wet ingredients into the dry and combine until smooth.

Heat the waffle iron, according to Owner's Manual. When the iron is hot, pour batter into the center of the lower half until 2/3 of the surface is covered. Close lid gently.

Cook until waffle stops steaming (about 4 minutes). Do not lift lid during baking! Lift the lid when the waffle is done and carefully pull away with a fork. If the waffle doesn't come off easily—cook a little longer.

Repeat with the reaming batter. You should be able to make 8 large waffles.

Serve hot with butter and syrup, confectioners sugar, fresh whipped cream of fruit topping!

INGREDIENTS

Makes 8 Large Waffles

2 cups all-purpose flour

1 Tablespoon baking powder

1/2 teaspoon salt

2 tablespoons sugar

1 3/4 cups milk

2 large eggs

6 Tablespoons vegetable oil or melted and cooled butter

Butter-Pecan Waffles

INGREDIENTS

Makes 8 Large Waffles

2 cups all-purpose flour

1 Tablespoon baking powder

1/2 teaspoon salt

1/4 cup firmly packed light brown sugar

3/4 cup pecans; finely chopped

1 3/4 cups milk

2 large eggs

6 Tablespoons vegetable oil

2 teaspoons Butter Flavoring

I first had these while I lived in Texas! They were so good I played around with recipes until I finally came up with one I liked. They are great with maple syrup or with a sautéed banana topping!

PREPARATION:

Use your food processor or mini chopper to chop the pecans very fine.

Sift the dry ingredients together in a medium or large mixing bowl. In a smaller bowl, mix the milk, eggs, oil and butter flavoring together until the eggs are completely mixed.

Pour the wet ingredients into the dry and combine until smooth.

Heat the waffle iron, according to Owner's Manual. When the iron is hot, pour batter into the center of the lower half until 2/3 of the surface is covered. Close lid gently.

Cook until waffle stops steaming (about 4 minutes). Do not lift lid during baking! Lift the lid when the waffle is done and carefully pull away with a fork. If the waffle doesn't come off easily–cook a little longer.

Repeat with the reaming batter. You should be able to make 8 large waffles.

Try serving these with Sautéed Banana Topping (see index for recipe location).

Ham & Cheese Waffles

These savory waffles are a change from the norm! They are especially good to serve for a brunch.

INGREDIENTS

Makes 8 Large Waffles

2 cups all-purpose flour

1 Tablespoon baking powder

1/2 teaspoon salt

2 tablespoons sugar

1 3/4 cups milk

2 large eggs

3/4 cup grated Swiss or Gruyere cheese

1 cup finely chopped ham

6 Tablespoons vegetable oil

PREPARATION:

Use the grating attachment of your Food Processor (or hand-held grater) to finely grate the cheese. Use the chopping blades and finely chop the ham.

Sift the dry ingredients together in a medium or large mixing bowl. In a smaller bowl, mix the milk, eggs, oil, cheese and ham together until the eggs are completely mixed.

Pour the wet ingredients into the dry and combine until smooth.

Heat the waffle iron, according to Owner's Manual. When the iron is hot, pour batter (see note below) into the center of the lower half until 2/3 of the surface is covered. Close lid gently.

Cook until waffle stops steaming (about 4 minutes). Do not lift lid during baking! Lift the lid when the waffle is done and carefully pull away with a fork. If the waffle doesn't come off easily—cook a little longer.

Repeat with the reaming batter. You should be able to make 8 large waffles.

NOTE:

Be sure and stir the batter well before spooning onto the waffle iron as the ham and cheese will settle to the bottom.

Serve these waffles with warm maple syrup on the side.

Appetizers, Snacks, Dips & Spreads

Party Reubens

INGREDIENTS

36 slices cocktail rye bread

1/4 - 1/2 cup Thousand Island dressing

1 8-ounce can sauerkraut; rinsed & drained well

1/4 pound thinly sliced corned beef; cut into 1" x 3" strips.

3/4 pound thin sliced Swiss cheese; cut into 2" x 2" squares.

These are really good—just make sure you make enough!

PREPARATION:

Preheat your convection oven to 400°.

Place the bread slices in a single layer on your work surface.

Place 1/2 - 1 tsp. of Thousand Island Salad dressing on each piece of bread; spread evenly.

Fold each strip of Corned Beef in thirds and place on top of dressing.

Use a fork and top beef with 1-2 teaspoons sauerkraut.

Place one square of cheese on top of each snack.

Using a cookie sheet or piece of aluminum foil that will fit your oven, place as many snacks as will comfortably fit.

Place onto the center rack of your oven and cook 6-8 minutes or until cheese is melted and beginning to brown.

Serve hot.

18

Party Time! Appetizers, Snacks, Dips & Spreads   ELECTRIC EATS

Pigs in Blankets

Such an easy thing to make that seems to please everyone!

PREPARATION:

Preheat Convection oven to 400°.

Pop open the can of rolls and separate into triangles; lay flat on your work surface.

Slit each hot dog lengthwise about halfway through the dog.

Unwrap and slice each piece of cheese into 4 strips.

Place 2 strips of cheese into the slit of the hot dog and place cheese-side up onto the widest part of crescent roll. Roll the hot dog in the crescent roll ending with the cheese up and the point of the roll on top.

Repeat with remaining hotdogs, cheese and rolls.

Place the pigs in blankets onto a greased cookie sheet or on a piece of aluminum pan.

Put on center rack of oven and cook 6-8 minutes or until rolls are golden brown.

Serve hot with mustard or ketchup.

PARTY TIP:

If you are making these for a large group, use the small cocktail wieners and cut the cheese and crescent rolls down to fit! Make and bake as directed above.

EVEN EASIER:

Use the cocktail wieners or hotdogs already stuffed with cheese!

INGREDIENTS

8 all-beef hotdogs

4 slices American cheese

1 can Pop-Open Crescent Rolls
(8 count)

ELECTRIC EATS Party Time! Appetizers, Snacks, Dips & Spreads

19

Party Cheese Dip

INGREDIENTS

1 8 oz. block cream cheese

1 8 oz. block Velveeta cheese

1/2 cup Blue cheese crumbles

3 thinly sliced green onions with tops

1 small jar chopped pimento; drained

2 tsp. garlic salt

2 tsp. Worcestershire sauce

I originally made up this recipe to demonstrate the power of the Bravetti hand mixer on HSN; however, you can use your food processor as well! Because this is one of my most requested demo recipes, I wanted to keep it in my newest book!

PREPARATION:

Use your Bravetti hand mixer with the traditional beaters to blend these ingredients into a smooth creamy dip. Serve with crackers and celery stalks.

PROCESSOR USE:

You can make this dip in your food processor or food prep center! Just use the dough blade and mix all the ingredients together on the lowest speed!

20

Party Time! Appetizers, Snacks, Dips & Spreads   ELECTRIC EATS

Artichoke Spinach Dip

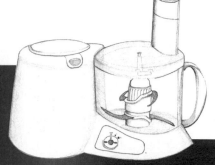

This recipe can be made using your food processor and baked in your convection oven! It also tastes so good I make it all the time, at home as well as on-air.

PREPARATION:

Using your chopping blade of your food processor, process artichokes until well chopped. Remove the chopping blade and insert the dough blade. Add the spinach, mayonnaise, cream cheese, Parmesan cheese, lemon juice and black pepper. Process until smooth and well blended.

Spread mixture into a 9" square or 9"x11" baking dish. Sprinkle evenly with the paprika. Cook for 20 minutes at 350° or until hot and bubbly.

Serve hot with Melba toast, crackers or Cheese Straws.

PARTY TIP:

For a large crowd, double the recipe and use your 3-quart slow cooker! Heat on high for 1 hour and then reduce heat to the keep warm setting; serve the dip directly from the slow cooker.

MAXI-BLEND USERS:

You can make this in your Maxi-Blend. However—make half at a time and just pulse, pulse, pulse! Do not just hold the top down as this mixture is thick and will burn out your motor!

INGREDIENTS

1 cup artichokes

1 10-ounce package frozen chopped spinach; thawed and drained

1 cup mayonnaise

1 8-ounce block cream cheese

1 cup grated Parmesan cheese

1 tablespoon lemon juice

1/2 teaspoon coarse ground black pepper

1/2 teaspoon paprika

E ELECTRIC EATS Party Time! Appetizers, Snacks, Dips & Spreads

21

Bruchetta

INGREDIENTS

4 medium Roma tomatoes

10 medium pitted black olives

1/2 small onion

2 Tablespoons capers; drained

2 cloves garlic; peeled

5-6 large basil leaves or 1 teaspoon dried basil

2 Tablespoons extra virgin light olive oil

1 loaf fresh baguette or thin French bread; sliced into 16 - 3/4" slices.

1/4 cup finely shredded or coarsely chopped parmesan cheese (optional).

This is one of my favorite appetizers to serve as it is easy and great tasting!

PREPARATION:

Using your Food Processor or Maxi-Blend, chop the garlic, onion and fresh basil until well minced.

Add the tomatoes, olives, capers and olive oil and pulse until coarsely chopped. Refrigerate at least one hour or up to three.

Preheat Convection Oven to 400°.

Choose a cookie sheet or piece of aluminum foil that will fit into your convection oven. Arrange as many slices of bread that will comfortably fit.

Top each slice of bread with 1-2 Tablespoons of the tomato mixture and top with a sprinkling parmesan cheese (if desired). The quantity you can make depends on how much topping you put on each slice. So judge accordingly to how many people you wish to serve!

Bake, on center rack, for 8-10 minutes or until bread is crispy around the edges.

22

Party Time! Appetizers, Snacks, Dips & Spreads   ELECTRIC EATS

Whole Roasted Garlic

It takes an hour to roast the garlic, but it can be made a week before using! Serve it hot or at room temperature with the Buttery Sun Dried Tomato Bread Chips or Cheese Straws; it's sure to be a hit!

INGREDIENTS

4 large heads garlic

1/4 cup extra virgin olive oil

1 tablespoon coarse salt

Crackers, sliced baguette or Buttery Sun Dried Tomato Bread Chips (next page)

PREPARATION:

Preheat your convection oven to 400°.

Use a sharp knife and slice off the tops of the garlic heads; discard.

Place the heads onto a large piece of aluminum foil. Drizzle the olive oil over the exposed garlic cloves and sprinkle with the salt.

Fold the aluminum foil over and seal to form and airtight pouch.

Place the pouch onto the center rack of your oven and bake for 1 hour. Remove and let cool. Remove garlic from foil and serve hot or refrigerate for up to one week.

If making ahead, let the garlic reach room temperature before serving

CONVECTION OVEN

Buttery Sun Dried Tomato Bread Chips

INGREDIENTS

1 baguette or long sourdough bread

3/4 cup extra virgin olive oil

4 sun dried oil-packed tomatoes; patted dry of oil

2 cloves garlic

1/2 teaspoon salt

3 tablespoons fresh parsley; minced

Make these to serve with dips, along with a Caesar salad or just as snacks!

PREPARATION:

Preheat Convection Oven to 375°.

Slice the bread into 1/8" thick slices.

Place the garlic and sun dried tomatoes into your Maxi-Blend or food processor and process until finely minced.

In a small sauté pan, heat the oil over medium heat. Add the garlic and tomatoes and heat until they sizzle but do not brown; remove from heat and stir in salt.

Quickly dip the bread into the oil mixture, or lightly brush the bread on both sides, and place on baking sheet or aluminum foil to fit your oven.

Bake 15 minutes or until golden brown. Place bread onto paper towels and sprinkle with parsley. Allow to cool.

Serve or store in an airtight container.

24

Party Time! Appetizers, Snacks, Dips & Spreads   ELECTRIC EATS

Italian Meatball Appetizers

These are a tasty addition to your party! Plus, they are easy to make using your food processor!

PREPARATION:

Preheat your convection oven to 450°.

Grease the broiler pan that came with your convection oven.

Using your food processor with the quad-blades, pulse the onion and garlic together until well minced.

Turn the processor to mid-speed and quickly drop the meat, one chunk at a time, down the food shoot, until all the meat is ground. Turn processor off and remove lid.

Pour the breadcrumbs, spaghetti sauce, cheese and egg evenly over the meat and replace the lid. Pulse the processor several times until everything is well mixed.

Remove lid and blades from processor.

Form the meat mixture into small meatballs; about 1 rounded Tablespoon each.   Place the meatballs on the greased broiler pan; you may have to do two batches depending on the size of your broiler pan.

Slide the broiler pan of meatballs into the center of your oven. Cook 15 minutes, turning once, or until done.

Stick toothpicks into the meatballs and serve on a platter with a dish of warmed spaghetti sauce.

INGREDIENTS

1 lb. eye of round roast or other lean beef; cut into large chunks

1 small onion

2 cloves garlic

1/2 cup seasoned bread crumbs

1/4 cup grated parmesan cheese

1/2 cup plain spaghetti or sauce (canned)

1 large egg

ELECTRIC EATS   Party Time! Appetizers, Snacks, Dips & Spreads

25

Pimento Cheese Spread

1 lb. Block Extra Sharp cheddar cheese

1/3 cup mayonnaise (homemade is best)

1 Tbsp. Vinegar

1/4 tsp. Dry mustard

1/4 tsp. Worcestershire

1/2 tsp. Salt

1/2 tsp. pepper

1 1/2 oz. Jar chopped pimento; drained

This is Chris Scanlon's favorite dip so I always try to make it on air when she is my show host!

PREPARATION:

Using the small shredding blade of your Food Processor, shred cheese. Remove shredding blade; insert dough blade.

In a small bowl, mix together the mayonnaise, vinegar, dry mustard, Worcestershire, salt and pepper until well blended. Add the mayonnaise mixture along with the pimentos to the cheese inside the food processor bowl.

Process the mixture on a medium speed for about 1 minute or until creamy.

Serve the spread with Buttery Sun Dried Tomato Bread, crackers, as a sandwich or stuffed into celery stalks.

26

Party Time! Appetizers, Snacks, Dips & Spreads   ELECTRIC EATS E

Zucchini & Carrot Nut Muffins

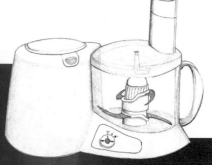

These moist muffins will soon be a family favorite!
This recipe can be made very quickly in your Food Processor.

PREPARATION:

Cut the zucchini and carrot into thirds and place into your Quad-Blade Food Processor; pulse several times until the mixture is well chopped. Add the remaining ingredients, in order listed, and process on low speed until well mixed.

Grease a 12-muffin tin or spray with non-stick spray. Fill each cup 2/3 with batter.

Preheat Conventional Oven to 400° or Convection Oven to 375°.

Bake for 13 to 16 minutes or until done.

IF YOU DO NOT HAVE A FOOD PROCESSOR:

Shred the zucchini and carrots. Chop the nuts.

In a large bowl, beat the egg until light and frothy. Mix in the oil and sugar.

Stir in the carrots, zucchini and vanilla. Combine the flour and remaining ingredients and stir into the egg mixture.

Bake as directed above.

INGREDIENTS

1 medium zucchini; ends trimmed

1 medium carrot; peeled & ends trimmed

1 large egg

1/2 cup vegetable oil

1 cups sugar

1 teaspoon vanilla

1 1/2 cups flour

1/2 teaspoon salt

1/2 teaspoon baking powder

1/2 teaspoon baking soda

1 teaspoon cinnamon

1/4 teaspoon nutmeg

1/2 cup walnuts

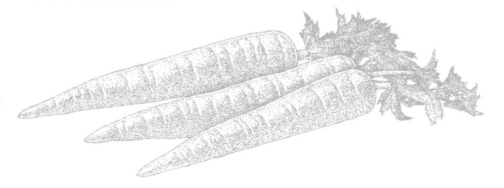

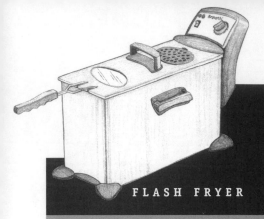

Asian-Style Chicken Wings

INGREDIENTS

1 1/2 pounds Chicken Wings; separated, washed and patted dry

Asian Wing Sauce:

1 cup hoi sin sauce

3/4 cup plum sauce

1/2 cup low-sodium soy sauce

1/3 cup white vinegar

1/4 cup honey

1 teaspoon dry ginger or 2 Tablespoons minced fresh ginger

1/4 cup toasted sesame seeds

This is a delightful change from the "hot wings" and just as easy! I prefer to flash fry these first and then bake them in the oven in the sauce.

PREPARATION:

Preheat your Bravetti Flash Fryer to 375°.

Using metal tongs, gently drop wings into lowered basket of fryer; do not overcrowd. Fry, with lid on, for 8 minutes or until golden brown. Drain on paper towels and place in non-stick baking dish.

Preheat your Convection Oven to 375°.

Mix wing sauce ingredients together and heat in small saucepan until warm. Pour desired amount of sauce over wings and bake in a 350° oven for 10-15 minutes.

Remove from pan, arrange on a platter and sprinkle with toasted sesame seeds. Serve with remaining sauce.

Party Tip: To prepare larger amounts, fry wings in 1 lb. increments, then place in 9 1/2" x 11" pan. The wing sauce is enough to generously coat about 3 pounds of wings.

BAKED ONLY METHOD:

If you do not want to fry the wings, simply place the uncooked wings on a baking sheet, baste with the sauce and roast 30 minutes. Turn, baste the other side and roast another 30 minutes.

Vegetable Spring Rolls

Spring rolls are fantastic! You can make a whole batch, fry some to eat now and then freeze the rest for a later day.

PREPARATION:

Put the noodles into a bowl and cover with boiling water. Let soak for 10 minutes. Drain and coarsely chop.

In a large skillet, heat oil over medium heat. Add garlic and ginger and cook until sizzling. Add scallions and cabbage. Cook, stirring frequently, until cabbage has wilted. Remove from heat and add carrots, Thai sauce and soy sauce. Mix well.

Preheat your Flash Fryer to 375°.

Place 1 spring roll on your work surface. Brush edges with egg white. Place 1 heaping Tablespoon of filling in center of wrapper. Roll the bottom of the wrapper diagonally over filling Fold in sides and roll up diagonally. Seal edges with egg white.

Repeat with remaining wrappers and filling.

Fry the spring rolls in batches and drain on paper towels. Serve with Sweet & Sour Sauce (on next page) or a Plum Sauce.

INGREDIENTS

1 ounce cellophane noodles

2 Tablespoons vegetable oil

3 cloves garlic; minced

1 inch piece peeled and grated fresh ginger or 1 teaspoon dried

6 scallions/green onions, including 1 inch of green on each onion; finely chopped

3 cups Chinese (Napa) cabbage; shredded.

3 medium carrots; peeled and grated

1/3 cup Thai sweet chili sauce

2 Tablespoons low-sodium soy sauce

18 frozen 8 1/2 x 8 1/2 spring roll wrappers; thawed

1 egg white; lightly beaten

Sweet and Sour Dipping Sauce

INGREDIENTS

2 tablespoons cornstarch

1/2 cup chicken broth

2 tablespoons soy sauce

2 tablespoons butter

1 cup chicken broth

3/4 cup pineapple juice

1/2 cup mild vinegar

1/4 cup brown sugar

1/4 cup granulated sugar

1/2 teaspoon salt

1/4 teaspoon ginger

Try this sauce as a dipping sauce for Spring Rolls, an addition to stir fry.

PREPARATION:

Make a paste of the cornstarch, 1/2 cup broth and soy sauce.

In a heavy pan, melt the butter over medium heat.

Add in the chicken broth and pineapple juice, cover and simmer 5 minutes. While mixture is bubbly, add the cornstarch paste and the remaining ingredients.

Simmer, stirring often until the mixture thickens slightly.

NOTE:

If you desire a thicker sauce, increase corn starch to 3 Tablespoons.

Nachos

Whether you make them bare bones or with all the trimmings, Nachos are always a crowd pleaser!
I am not listing quantity with the ingredients because it depends greatly on the size of your pan and your taste preferences!

PREPARATION:

Preheat Convection Oven to 400°.

Place the tortilla chips on a baking sheet in a semi-single layer (it's OK if they all overlap). Heavily sprinkle cheddar cheese over all and scatter jalapenos to taste.

Bake on center rack 5-7 minutes or until cheese is melted.

BETTER NACHOS:

Layer the chips and then top with:

Shredded Cheddar Cheese
Shredded Monterey Jack Cheese
Sliced Black Olives
Finely chopped Onion
Jalapeno Slices
Salsa

Bake as directed above.

MACHO NACHOS:

Layer the chips and then top with:

Refried beans, Black beans or Chili
Finely chopped Onion
Shredded Cheddar Cheese
Shredded Monterey Jack Cheese

Bake as directed above. Remove from oven and top with:

Shredded Lettuce
Sliced Black Olives
Sour Cream
Salsa or Chopped Tomatoes
Sliced Jalapeno Peppers
Guacamole

INGREDIENTS

Basic Nachos:
Tortilla Chips
Shredded Cheddar Cheese
Pickled Jalapeno peppers

Better Nachos:
Shredded Cheddar Cheese
Shredded Monterey Jack Cheese
Sliced Black Olives
Finely chopped Onion
Jalapeno Slices
Salsa

Macho Nachos:
Refried beans, Black beans or Chili
Finely chopped Onion
Shredded Cheddar Cheese
Shredded Monterey Jack Cheese
Shredded Lettuce
Sliced Black Olives
Sour Cream
Salsa or Chopped Tomatoes
Sliced Jalapeno Peppers
Guacamole

Spicy Fresh Salsa

INGREDIENTS

6 medium plum tomatoes; ends trimmed and halved lengthwise

1/2 medium-large white onion; peeled and halved

1 medium jalapeno; stem and seeds removed

1/2 bunch cilantro; large stems removed

1/2 teaspoon Salt

1/2 teaspoon cumin

1 51/2-ounce can spicy V-8 juice

It there anything as good as homemade salsa? Especially if the tomatoes are from your own garden! I serve this salsa with chips, on nachos and other Mexican food and over omelets.

PREPARATION:

Place the chopping blade of your food processor into the processor bowl. Arrange all ingredients evenly around the bowl.

Use the pulse button intermittently to chop mixture to desired consistency.

MAXI-BLEND:

If using your maxi-blend to make salsa, cut the ingredients back 25%. Use 4 tomatoes, 1/4 onion, etc. Make sure the tomatoes and onions are place in from the bottom up; be careful not to cut yourself on the blade! On air, I do not precut the tomatoes, however if you use large ones, cut them so the will easily reach the bottom of the bowl.

32

Party Time! Appetizers, Snacks, Dips & Spreads   ELECTRIC EATS E

Guacamole

INGREDIENTS

I absolutely love guacamole! Many restaurants try to make the avocados go a long way by adding sour cream or, heaven forbid, mayonnaise. I prefer to really taste the avocados so I use neither. If you want to serve this in the winter and avocados are very expensive and you need to make a lot, please use sour cream and never mayonnaise!

2 large ripe avocados; peeled and seed removed

1/2 lemon

1/2 teaspoon cayenne pepper

1/2 teaspoon Worcestershire sauce

1/4 teaspoon salt, or more to taste

1 tablespoon grated onion (optional)

2 tablespoons tomato, seeded and finely chopped (optional)

PREPARATION:

Peel, remove seed and slice or cube avocado; put into a small mixing bowl.

Add spices and squeeze lemon over all being mindful of the lemon's seeds.

Mix all ingredients, except tomato, together until creamy using the traditional beaters of your Hand Mixer, or mash with a fork.

Gently fold in the tomatoes. Serve at once or if you need to refrigerate it, place a layer of plastic wrap directly on the guacamole (not just the top of the bowl) to prevent it from browning.

E ELECTRIC EATS *Party Time! Appetizers, Snacks, Dips & Spreads*

33

Roasted Garlic Spread

INGREDIENTS

1 head roasted garlic
(see recipe index)

8 ounces cream cheese; cut into
4 pieces

5 green onion tops (about 2 inches
from each onion)

4 tablespoons half and half

I love this spread, but it kills my breath! it's a good idea to surround this dip with fresh parsley and encourage guests to nibble on a bit after the dip! This will make the non-dip-eating guests very happy!!

PREPARATION:

Place the cream cheese, onion tops and half and half into your food processor or Maxi-Blend. Squeeze the garlic cloves from their skins on top of cheese and cream.

Process, using the pulse or a low speed, until smooth.

Serve at room temperature with crackers, Buttery Sun Dried Tomato Bread or Cheese Straws.

Mango Salsa

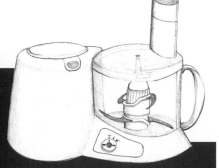

This is such a great change from the ordinary salsa. Besides being good on chips, it is excellent served along side fish dishes, particularly grilled fish.

INGREDIENTS

4 green onions

1/3 bunch cilantro; large stems removed

1 1-inch piece peeled fresh ginger

2 cups mango flesh (about 2 mangos)

2 Tablespoons Lime Juice

2 Tablespoons light brown sugar

2 Tablespoons low-sodium soy sauce

PREPARATION:

Place all ingredients into your food processor or Maxi-Blend. Using your pulse button, rapidly pulse until all the ingredients are chopped coarsely.

Refrigerate until ready to use. Serve with tortilla chips.

Salsa must be used within 12 hours of making

TIP:

If you cannot find fresh mango, there is usually jarred available in the produce section of your grocery. If not, look in the frozen fruit section! I often use frozen instead just so I don't have to peel the mango!

VARIATION:

Try adding a little kiwi to this salsa!

E ELECTRIC EATS   *Party Time! Appetizers, Snacks, Dips & Spreads*

35

Avocado & Corn Salsa

INGREDIENTS

1 large ripe avocado

2 Tablespoons lime juice

1/2 cup frozen corn kernels; thawed and patted dry

4 green onions; white and light green parts thinly sliced

1 4.5-ounce can chopped chilies

1 teaspoon cumin

1 1/2 teaspoon kosher salt

1/4 cup chopped fresh cilantro

I love to try new dips, and so do your guests and family! Try making this salsa just to change things up a bit!

PREPARATION:

Peel, remove seed and coarsely chop the avocado. Place into a glass bowl and immediately toss with the lime juice.

Add the remaining ingredients and gently mix together. Serve immediately or place a layer of saran wrap directly on mixture and store in the refrigerator. This should be served within 2 hours of making.

36

Party Time! Appetizers, Snacks, Dips & Spreads   ELECTRIC EATS

Crab Rangoon

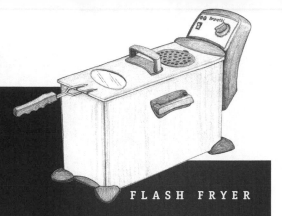

INGREDIENTS

8 ounces cream cheese

1 6-ounce can lump crab meat; drained

1/4 cup Confectioner's sugar

1/4 teaspoon salt

1/4 teaspoon Chinese five-spice powder

50 wonton wrappers

1 large egg

4 teaspoons water

I love these! I never could find a recipe I liked, so I made up my own! These turn out perfect if you use your Flash Fryer. Serve them with the vegetable spring rolls and a sweet and sour dipping sauce for a great Asian appetizer tray.

PREPARATION:

Preheat your Flash Fryer to highest setting.

Mix all ingredients together, in a medium bowl, until creamy and smooth. Mix egg and water together in small bowl until frothy.

Working on a smooth dry surface, lay out 12 wonton wrappers. Put 1 well-rounded teaspoon filling on the center of each wonton.

Working one at a time, lightly moisten all four edges of the wonton with the egg/water mixture. Bring two opposite points together into the center. Bring a third point into the center, sealing the two flat edges that are formed. Bring the final point into the center also sealing the flat edges. The flat edges should form and "X" on the top. Lightly push down so the bottom is somewhat flat. Lay on a plate. Repeat with remaining wontons and filling.

Makes 40-50 depending on the amount of filling you use in each one!

Drop the filled wontons, "X" up, into the hot oil; basket should already be lowered. Do not over crowd. Fry 4 minutes or until golden brown. Drain and serve immediately.

TIP:

It is very important to keep your work surface, and your hands, dry and clean. It is hard to work with a wet wonton, so limit the amount of egg you brush around the edge and clean your work surface often!

 ELECTRIC EATS ■ Party Time! Appetizers, Snacks, Dips & Spreads

37

FOOD PROCESSOR

Shrimp Dip

INGREDIENTS

12 ounces cream cheese; softened

1 cup Thousand Island salad dressing

1/2 cup mayonnaise

2 pounds frozen baby salad shrimp; thawed, rinsed and patted dry

6-8 green onions; whites and light green parts thinly sliced (about 1 cup)

4 teaspoons Tabasco Sauce

1 Tablespoon seasoned salt (home-made or store bought)

1 Tablespoon prepared horseradish

I like this dip! I think it has a great combination of flavors that make you go back and back to the dip bowl!

PREPARATION:

Use the dough blade of your food processor or your hand mixer and beat together the cream cheese, salad dressing, mayonnaise, green onions, Tabasco sauce, seasoned salt and horseradish.

Gently stir in the shrimp. Chill, covered, for 6-8 hours.

Serve with assorted party crackers.

Smoked Salmon Spread

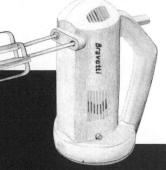

HAND MIXER

INGREDIENTS

I originally made up this spread for bagels. However, it is so good I often serve it with Wheat Thins at parties!

2 8-ounce blocks cream cheese

1 3-ounce foil package salmon

2 Tablespoons chopped fresh dill

1/2 teaspoon liquid smoke

1/4 teaspoon salt

1 teaspoon lemon juice

PREPARATION:

Place all the ingredients together in a medium mixing bowl. Use your hand mixer first on low speed to blend and the on high speed for a minute to get it light and fluffy.

Serve with Wheat Thins, bagel chips or Melba toast.

ELECTRIC EATS Party Time! Appetizers, Snacks, Dips & Spreads

39

Mexican Cheese Spread

INGREDIENTS

1 8-ounce block Velveeta cheese

1 8-ounce block cream cheese

1 10-ounce can Rotel chopped tomatoes with chilies; drained

1/2 teaspoon cumin

1/2 teaspoon coriander

1/4 teaspoon salt

1/4 teaspoon garlic powder

1/4 teaspoon cayenne pepper

This is a cold twist to the hot-cheese dip everyone is used to. I think it's better suited for outdoor summer parties!

PREPARATION:

Place all the ingredients together in a medium mixing bowl. Use your hand mixer first on low speed to blend and the on high speed for a minute to get it light and fluffy.

Serve with Fritos or tortilla chips.

Cheese Straws

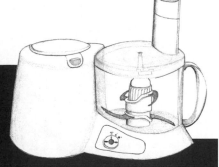

These are very good alone or with a dip! They may seem like a lot of work, but they are soooo much better than the store-bought breadsticks that it is definitely worth the effort!

PREPARATION:

Install the dough hook into your Food Processor.

Sift the flour and salt into processor bowl. Place on lid and turn to medium speed. Drop the butter down the food shoot one tablespoon at a time and process until the mixture becomes very grainy.

Add the cheese and half the egg and process until a dough forms.

Remove blade and store dough in refrigerator 30 minutes.

Preheat Convection Oven to 400°.

Roll out the dough on a floured surface to form a rectangle of 1/4 -inch thickness. Cut into 3" x 1/2 " strips. Twist and place on baking sheet.

Brush the straws with the remaining egg and sprinkle half with poppy seeds and half with toasted sesame seeds.

Bake 10-15 minutes or until golden brown. Serve hot or at room temperature.

INGREDIENTS

Makes About 24

1 cup flour

1/8 teaspoon salt

1/4 cup butter; cold and cut into tablespoons

1/2 cup finely shredded sharp cheddar cheese

1 egg; beaten

Poppy seeds and toasted sesame seeds

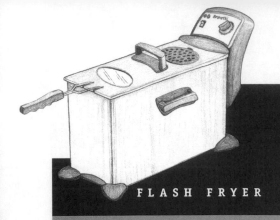

Parmesan Fritters

INGREDIENTS

1/4 cup butter

2/3 cup water

1/2 cup plus 6 teaspoons flour; sifted

2 eggs; beaten

1 teaspoon chopped fresh parsley

1/2 cup grated Parmesan Cheese

1/4 cup grated sharp Cheddar Cheese

1/2 teaspoon coarsely ground black pepper

Salt to taste

This recipe makes about 16 small fritters so if you are having a large group, consider doubling the recipe as they are very tasty!

PREPARATION:

Preheat your Flash Fryer to 375°.

In a large non-stick pot, melt butter over medium heat. Add water and bring to a boil.

Add the flour and stir quickly with a wooden spoon until the mixture pulls away from the sides of the pot. Reduce heat to low and vigorously beat in the eggs, a little at a time. Stir in cheeses, parsley and salt and pepper. Continue stirring until cheese has melted.

Carefully drop walnut-sized spoonfuls of batter into the fryer, being careful not to overcrowd, and fry 2-3 minutes or until puffed and golden brown.

42

Party Time! Appetizers, Snacks, Dips & Spreads   ELECTRIC EATS

Coconut Chicken Satay & Peanut Sauce

This is a very popular appetizer at upscale restaurants across the country. It is also very good! If you have a crowd you would like to impress, this is the thing to serve. Don't for get the sauce—it makes the dish.

PREPARATION:

In a measuring cup or small mixing bowl, combine all of the marinade ingredients. Pour into the bag with the chicken. Turn the bag to coat the chicken thoroughly.   Marinate in the refrigerator for 1 – 4 hours.

Remove the chicken from the bag and pat off excess marinade. Weave the chicken onto long wooden skewers.

Preheat Convection oven to 400° on the grill setting.

Place the skewers lengthwise onto the broiler pan that came with your convection oven. The skewer ends should sit up on the pan's edge keeping the chicken from laying flat onto the pan; if not, spray the pan with nonstick cooking spray.

Place the rack into the oven, at mid height, and cook for 5-6 minutes. Turn the skewers over and continue cooking another 8-10 minutes or until the chicken is beginning to brown on the edges. Top with toasted coconut. Serve with the Peanut Sauce recipe on the next page.

INGREDIENTS

1 pound boneless, skinless chicken breasts

1/2 cup toasted coconut

15 long wooden skewers

Marinade:

1/4 cup unsweetened coconut milk

2 Tablespoons low-sodium soy sauce

1/2 cup fresh cilantro leaves

1 Tablespoons extra virgin olive oil

1 Tablespoons lime juice

1 Tablespoon firmly packed light brown sugar

4 dashes Tabasco Sauce

Peanut Sauce

INGREDIENTS

1 cup chicken broth

1/2 cup unsweetened coconut milk

1 cup smooth peanut butter

1/4 cup firmly packed light brown sugar

1/4 cup low sodium soy sauce

1/2 teaspoon ground ginger

1/4 teaspoon ground cumin

Use this sauce with the Chicken Satay on the preceding page or as an accompaniment to grilled shrimp.

PREPARATION:

Stir all ingredients together in a 2-qt. saucepan. Bring the mixture to a boil. Reduce heat and simmer for 10 minutes, stirring until smooth.

Serve immediately or store in the refrigerator, in an air-tight container, for up to 3 days. Reheat by adding a little chicken broth if needed or serve cold straight from the fridge!

Beef Empanadas (Turnovers)

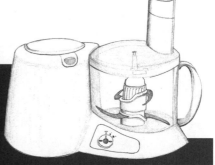

These are really yummy!

PREPARATION:

Place the beef into a saucepan, cover with water, and bring to a boil. Reduce heat and simmer until tender; about 45 minutes. Drain, reserving the broth.

Grind the meat in your Food Processor.

Combine the ground meat, raisins, applesauce, sugar, cinnamon, salt and pecans in a stockpot and mix well. Add enough of the reserved broth to thoroughly moisten the mixture. Bring to a simmer and cook 15 minutes, adding additional broth if mixture becomes dry. Remove from heat and let stand until cool.

Insert the dough blade into your Food processor and add flour, sugar, baking powder and salt. Turn processor on a low speed and add the shortening through the food shoot; process until crumbly. Turn the processor to a medium speed and add the egg. Slowly add the water until the mixture forms a ball (you may not need all of the water).

Roll the dough, on a lightly floured surface, until it is 1/8-inch thick. Cut with a biscuit cutter, re-rolling dough as necessary, until you have 25-27 rounds.

Preheat your Flash Fryer to 375°.

Fill each dough round with meat mixture. Fold the dough over, forming a half-circle. Pinch the edges or crimp with a fork to completely seal the edge.

Fry the empanadas, in batches, about 4 minutes or until browned.

INGREDIENTS

Filling:
1 1/2 lbs. beef chuck
3/4 cup raisins
1 1/2 cups applesauce
3/4 cup sugar
1/2 teaspoon cinnamon
1/2 teaspoon salt
1/3 cup chopped pecans

Dough:
2 1/4 cups flour
3 teaspoons sugar
3/4 teaspoon baking powder
3/4 teaspoon salt
2 Tablespoons shortening
1 medium egg
3/4 cup water

Oysters Casino

INGREDIENTS

5 slices bacon

2 cups rock salt (you can use kosher salt if you can find rock salt)

3/4 cup unsalted butter

1/2 cup (6-8) green onions; white and light green parts thinly sliced

1/4 cup sweet red pepper; finely chopped

1/3 cup fresh parsley leaves; chopped

2 Tablespoons dried bread crumbs

2 Tablespoons lemon juice

Salt and fresh ground black pepper to taste

24 oysters on the half shell

Yum, yum, yum—that's all I can say about these! This recipe makes 24 but can easily be made larger or smaller to fit your crowd!

PREPARATION:

Preheat convection oven to 450°. Spread the rock salt onto the bottom of a pan large enough to hold all the oysters (split into 2 pans if your oven will not hold a large pan).

Wash the oyster, in its shell, and blot the excess liquid away; be careful not to puncture the oyster. Slide a knife through the mussel attaching the oyster to the shell so it can be easily removed. Place the oysters in their shells on top of the rock salt.

Cut the raw bacon strips into small pieces. Fry, in a small fry pan, until about half-way cooked. Remove bacon and let drain on paper towels. Wipe out pan and melt the butter.

Add to the melted butter in the pan, the onions and red pepper. Quickly sauté for 1-2 minutes; remove from heat. Add to the pan the parsley, bread-crumbs, lemon juice, salt and pepper. Stir to blend with the onions and peppers.

Spoon equal amounts of this mixture over each oyster and top with a couple bacon pieces. Bake until the oyster is heated through and the bacon is sizzling brown; about 6 minutes.

TIP:

If you plan to make this often, save the shells to use again with already-shucked fresh oysters!

46

Party Time! Appetizers, Snacks, Dips & Spreads   ELECTRIC EATS

SUPPER TIME!
ENTRÉES FOR ALL

Rotisserie Roast Beef

CONVECTION OVEN

INGREDIENTS

3 lb. Sirloin tip or eye of round roast (or the size that will fit to your oven)

1 Tbsp. olive oil

1 Tbsp. rosemary leaves

2 tsp. thyme

1/2 tsp. rubbed sage

1 tsp. oregano

2 tsp. garlic salt

1 tsp. coarsely ground black pepper

If you own a rotisserie, like the one I present on HSN, you will love this recipe. It makes the perfect roasts and a beautiful presentation for a dinner party.

PREPARATION:

Skewer the beef onto the rotisserie prongs; lock end into place. Rub the entire surface of the beef with the olive oil. Mix the remaining seasoning together and sprinkle evenly over roast pressing the seasonings lightly into the roast for better sticking.

Insert rotisserie attachment into the oven. Turn the oven to 450, rotisserie and stay on settings. Turn the convection feature on. Cook for 30 minutes then reduce heat to 375, turn off convection feature and continue cooking until desired internal temperature is achieved; about 40 minutes more for medium-rare.

Carefully remove rotisserie from oven and set onto a large cutting board. Disengage the end and slide, using a fork, the beef off the prongs and onto the board. Wait 5-10 minutes before cutting.

Serve with oven roasted potatoes and:

Creamy Horseradish Sauce
1/2 cup sour cream
2 tbsp. prepared horseradish
1 tbsp. dried parsley flakes
1 tsp. Worcestershire sauce

Home-Style Meatloaf

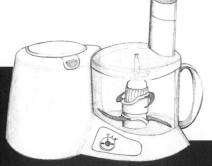

INGREDIENTS

3 lbs. lean ground beef

1 medium onion; finely chopped

1 medium green bell pepper; finely chopped

1 clove garlic; minced

1/4 cup ketchup, plus extra or the top

2 large eggs

2 tablespoon Worcestershire sauce

1 teaspoon Salt

1/4 teaspoon black pepper

3 slices white bread; torn into small pieces

1 tablespoon milk

This tried and true recipe can be made with ground beef and the dough hooks of your mixer or large cuts of meat to grind in your Food Processor (see next page). I do both demonstrations on HSN and it always works beautifully!

PREPARATION:

Preheat oven to 375°.

Moisten the bread pieces in the milk.

In a large mixing bowl, divide and layer the meat with the moistened bread-crumbs so you have about 3 layers. Add the onion, peppers, garlic, ketchup, eggs, Worcestershire sauce, salt and pepper. Use the dough hooks of your mixer and blend the ingredients together on the lowest speed. If you don't have my Bravetti mixer, you'll have to use your hands! Just be gentle with the mixture so you don't toughen the meat.

Form the meat into a loaf and place it in a lightly greased 9x9-inch or 7 1/2 x 10-inch baking dish. Cover loosely with foil and bake for 45 minutes.

Remove the meatloaf from the oven; carefully pour off the excess fat. Spread a little ketchup on the meatloaf and return to oven to bake, uncovered, another 15 minutes or until a meat thermometer reads 160° when inserted into the middle. Do not overcook; you do not want a dry meatloaf!

E ELECTRIC EATS   Supper Time! Entrées for All!

49

Home-Style Meatloaf– in your Food Processor

INGREDIENTS

1 1/2 lbs. lean beef roast; cut into large chunks

1/2 medium onion; peeled and halved

1/2 medium green bell pepper; seeds and membrane removed and halved

1/4 cup ketchup, plus extra for the top

1 large egg

1 tablespoon Worcestershire sauce

1/2 teaspoon Salt

1/4 teaspoon black pepper

1/4 cup dried bread crumbs

You can make meatloaf in your Food Processor using lean cuts of beef, but you have to limit the quantity of meat. You may need to make two batches if you have a hungry family! You can form the two batches into one large loaf or make two small loaves.

PREPARATION:

Preheat oven to 375°.

Place your quad-blades into your Food processor. Add the onion and pepper; pulse two times. Turn the processor on a medium-high speed and drop the meat chunks, one at a time, down the food shoot.

Turn processor off, remove lid and add remaining ingredients.

Replace lid and pulse two or three times or until all ingredients are mixed.

Form the meat into a loaf and place it in a lightly greased 9x9-inch or 7 1/2 x 10-inch baking dish. Cover loosely with foil and bake for 45 minutes.

Remove the meatloaf from the oven; carefully pour off the excess fat. Spread a little ketchup on the meatloaf and return to oven to bake, uncovered, another 15 minutes or until a meat thermometer reads 160° when inserted into the middle. Do not overcook; you do not want a dry meatloaf!

Italian-Style Meatloaf

INGREDIENTS

1 1/2 lbs. lean ground beef

1 small onion; peeled and halved

3 cloves garlic; peeled

1/2 green bell pepper; seeds and membrane removed

1/2 cup meatless spaghetti sauce (jarred or homemade)

1 large egg

2 tablespoons Italian seasoning

1/2 teaspoon Salt

1/4 teaspoon black pepper

1/4 teaspoon crushed red pepper

1/3 cup dried seasoned bread crumbs

3/4 cup shredded mozzarella cheese

These directions are for use with your Food Processor. If you do not want to use your Processor, simply use pre-ground beef and mince all other ingredients by hand! Please note that you may need to double this recipe for a large crowd, however you must process each batch separately as to not over-work your machine!

PREPARATION:

Preheat oven to 375°.

Place your quad-blades into your Food processor. Add the onion, garlic and pepper; pulse two times. Turn the processor on a medium-high speed and drop the meat chunks, one at a time, down the food shoot.

Turn processor off, remove lid and add 1/3 cup of the spaghetti sauce, 1/2 cup of the cheese and the remaining ingredients.

Replace lid and pulse two or three times or until all ingredients are mixed.

Form the meat into a loaf and place it in a lightly greased 9x9-inch or 7 1/2 x 10-inch baking dish. Cover loosely with foil and bake for 45 minutes.

Remove the meatloaf from the oven and carefully pour off the excess fat. Spread the remaining spaghetti sauce on the top and sprinkle with remaining cheese. Bake another 15 minutes or until a meat thermometer reads 160°.

FOOD PROCESSOR

Stuffed Peppers

INGREDIENTS

6 medium yellow, green or red peppers

1 1/2 lbs. chuck roast; cut into large chunks or pre-ground chuck

1/2 cup onion

3 cloves garlic

1 teaspoon salt

1 1/2 cups cooked long grain white rice

1 -2 ounce jar chopped pimento

1 -15 ounce can tomato sauce

1 Tablespoon Worcestershire Sauce

1/2 teaspoon oregano

1 teaspoon basil

2 cups shredded sharp cheddar cheese

Stuffed peppers are one of my favorite dishes. My son Max, however, doesn't like peppers so I usually only stuff four peppers and leave the remaining filling for his dinner!

PREPARATION:

Preheat Convection Oven to 375° on Bake.

Cut of the tops of the peppers. Remove seeds and large membrane.

Using the quad-blades in your Food Processor, pulse together the onion and garlic cloves until chopped fine. With the processor running at medium-high speed, drop the chunks of beef, one at a time, into the food shoot and process until ground.

In a medium skillet, cook the beef, onions, garlic and salt together until beef is browned. Add the rice, pimentos and 1 cup of the cheese and mix well.

Combine the tomato sauce, Worcestershire Sauce, oregano and basil. Pour 3/4 of the sauce into the meat mixture and stir well.

Fill each pepper with the meat filling (about 1 1/4 cup per pepper).

Arrange the peppers in an oven-safe dish and cook 30 minutes. Top the peppers with the remaining sauce and the cheese and bake another 15 minutes or until peppers are tender and cheese is melted.

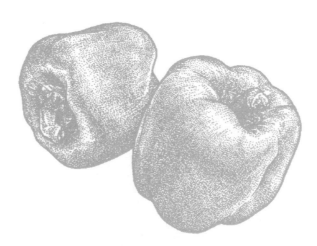

52

Supper Time! Entrées for All! ELECTRIC EATS E

Rotisserie Roasted Prime Rib Roast

Superb and guaranteed to impress!

PREPARATION:

Peel the garlic and cut each clove into thirds, lengthwise. Using a sharp, thin knife, cut 12 slits evenly spaced on the fat of the roast. Poke a piece of garlic into each slit.

Rub the entire surface of the roast with olive oil. Evenly sprinkle the salt and pepper over the entire roast.

Load the roast on the spit, starting at the meaty end of the roast, maneuvering the spit rods (if the spit is a double-rod assembly) between the bones. Make sure the weight is evenly distributed on the spit.

Place the broiler or drip pan under the roast and add 1 cup water to the pan (this will be your drippings for your Au Jus). Place the roast into the oven and turn the oven to 450°. Roast for 30 minutes and then reduce heat to 375°.

Continue roasting until the internal temperature is 140° for rare (18 minutes per pound) to 160° for medium (20 minutes per pound). I do not recommend cooking the roast beyond 160° at the center because the roast may dry out. Remove the roast from the spit rod, cover loosely with aluminum foil and allow to rest 10-15 minutes before carving.

To carve, slice along the bones to remove them, then place the roast on a carving board and cut into slices of desired thickness.

If you do not have a rotisserie oven: Prepare as directed above and place on a roasting rack atop a pan with 1/4-inch water. Bake according to temperatures directed above.

Serve with Au Jus (next page) or Creamy Horseradish Sauce (see index).

INGREDIENTS

3-5 pound bone-in prime rib roast (depending on the size of your rotisserie)

4 cloves garlic; peeled

2 Tablespoons extra virgin olive oil

2 teaspoons coarse ground black pepper

3 teaspoons kosher or sea salt

Au Jus for Prime Rib Roasts

INGREDIENTS

Drippings from the pan

3 cups beef stock (fresh or made with Better than Bouillon brand beef base

Salt and fresh ground pepper to taste

Make this gravy while the roast is resting before carving!

PREPARATION:

Skim the fat from the drippings and pour the drippings into a medium saucepan.

Add the stock and bring to a boil. Simmer for 10 minutes, taste and add salt and pepper if needed.

TASTE TIP:

Substitute 1/2 cup of the water with red wine and add some herbs that you like!

Steak & Cheese Hoagies

These may not be as good as you get in Philly, but they aren't bad!

PREPARATION:

Preheat Convection Oven to 400° on bake.

Peel the onion, cut off both ends and cut in half lengthwise. Working end to end, cut into very thin slices.

Cut off the top of the pepper and remove seeds and membrane. Cut into thin strips.

Cut the steaks, across the grain, into 1/2 -inch strips. Cut those strips into 1-inch pieces.

Heat 1 Tablespoon oil and 2 Tablespoons butter in a medium sauté pan over medium heat. Add beef and cook until meat is done. Drain meat, transfer to a small dish, set aside. Wipe out pan.

Return pan to heat and add the remaining oil and butter. Add onions and cook 3-4 minutes. Add peppers and mushrooms and continue cooking, stirring often, until all veggies are tender.

Return beef to the pan and add Worcestershire Sauce, salt and pepper. Cook until heated through. Remove from heat.

Split the hoagie rolls and fill with the meat, peppers and onions. Place 2 slices of cheese on each.

Heat hoagies in oven until cheese melts.

INGREDIENTS

1 lb. very thinly sliced top round steak (minute steak)

1 medium sweet onion

1 small green or red pepper

1/2 lb. white mushrooms; thinly sliced

1 Tablespoon Worcestershire Sauce

1/2 teaspoon salt

1/4 teaspoon coarse black pepper

2 Tablespoons Vegetable Oil

4 Tablespoons Butter

4 hoagie rolls

8 slices Provolone Cheese

Cheesy Shepard's Pie

INGREDIENTS

1 lb. ground chuck

1 tablespoons butter

1 small onion; finely chopped

1 8-ounce bag frozen peas and carrots

1 cup double strength beef broth

2 teaspoons flour

1 tablespoon Worcestershire sauce

1/2 teaspoon salt

1/2 teaspoon coarse ground black pepper

2 tablespoons ketchup

3 cups mashed potatoes; instant or homemade

1 1/2 cups sharp cheddar cheese; shredded

A couple of years ago, I went to London several times to work on another shopping channel. While there, I fell in love with the Shepard's Pie. Although my version is a bit Americanized, it really hits the spot on a cold, rainy day and makes me think of Pub fare!

PREPARATION:

Preheat Convection Oven to 375° on the bake setting.

In a large heavy skillet, over medium heat, brown beef. Drain and set aside. Wipe out the pan and melt 2 tablespoons butter over medium heat. Stir in the onions and sauté gently for 2-3 minutes. Cook the frozen peas and carrots in lightly salted boiling water for 2 minutes, drain and add to the onions. Cook for another 1-2 minutes.

In a measuring cup or small bowl, whisk together the canned beef broth with the flour until blended. Pour over the vegetables. Stir in the Worcestershire sauce and the ketchup. Bring to a gentle boil, cover, reduce heat and cook for 20 minutes. Add the beef and mix well. Spread the beef and vegetable mixture into the bottom a slightly greased 8x8-inch oven-safe glass baking dish.

Spread the hot mashed potatoes over all. Top with cheese. Place into the preheated oven and bake 20-30 minutes or until potatoes and cheese are lightly browned and the edges look bubbly.

Savory Garlic Marinated Steaks

This is one of the best marinades I know! The longer you marinade, the better, and tenderer, the steaks are so marinade these Friday night for a Saturday Night cookout!
For the purpose of this book and the Bravetti products, I am using the broiler. However, I like it grilled better!

PREPARATION:

In a glass bowl, combine all the ingredients for the marinade. Pour the marinade into a zip-top plastic bag and add the steaks. Squeeze as much air out as you can and place into the refrigerator for 24-48 hours.

Preheat the broiler setting of your Bravetti convection oven to 400°; make sure you leave the door cracked!

Lightly oil your broiler pan and position the steaks on top. Position the pan mid-height in your oven. Broil, 5-7 minutes per side or until internal temperature reaches at least 145°.

Outdoor Grill Cooking: Preheat grill to medium-high heat. Grill the steaks 7-8 minutes per side or until internal temperature reaches at least 145°.

INGREDIENTS

2 1/2-pound beef steaks; I use rib eye, but strip steaks, t-bones or porterhouse work fine!

Marinade:
1/2 cup balsamic vinegar
1/4 cup low sodium soy sauce
3 Tablespoons minced garlic
2 Tablespoons light brown sugar
2 Tablespoons olive oil
2 teaspoons coarse ground pepper
2 teaspoons Worcestershire Sauce
1 teaspoon onion powder
1/2 teaspoon koshor salt
1/2 teaspoon liquid smoke flavoring
1 pinch cayenne pepper

Best-Ever Slow Cooker Pot Roast

INGREDIENTS

3-4 lb. round, chuck or boneless pot roast

2 Tbsp. vegetable oil

1/2 cup good red wine

1 clove garlic, minced

1 medium onion, coarsely chopped

1 Tbsp. Worcestershire sauce

1 Tbsp. ketchup

1 Tbsp. Better Than Bouillon beef bouillon base

1 tsp. salt

1 tsp. coarse ground black pepper

1 tsp. celery salt

1 cup hot water

1/2 lb. Baby carrots

10 small red potatoes

1 lb. Whole medium mushrooms

2 stalks celery with leaves, cut into 1 inch pieces

1 Tbsp. cornstarch or potato starch

1/4 cup cold water

This is my slow-cooker pot roast demonstration recipe! This always gets eaten before I can bring it home!

PREPARATION:

Heat oil in a large heavy skillet over medium-low heat. Using long tongs, carefully brown roast; about 1 minute on each side and end. Remove roast and set inside your 7 Qt. Slow cooker.

Add wine to the skillet and scrape bottom with spatula. Add onion and garlic, simmer 1 minute. Add next the next 7 ingredients; stir. Pour mixture over roast. Cover and cook in the slow cooker on low for 5-6 hours or on high for 3-4 hours. Arrange the vegetables around the roast and slow cook another 2 1/2 hours on low.

Remove roast and vegetables to a large platter; cover with foil to keep warm.

FOR GRAVY:

Transfer the liquid to a saucepan and bring to a boil. In a small bowl or cup mix cornstarch and water together, pour into bubbling liquid. Stir until gravy thickens; pour over roast and vegetables.

SEE RECIPES ON PAGES 4, 5, 14

SEE RECIPE ON PAGE 11

SEE RECIPES ON PAGES 22, 23, 24, 41, 46

SEE RECIPES ON PAGES 28, 29, 30, 37, 43, 44

SEE RECIPES ON PAGES 32, 33, 36, 65

SEE RECIPES ON PAGES 53, 54, 68

SEE RECIPES ON PAGES 116, 118, 119, 125, 126, 127

SEE RECIPE ON PAGE 129

Slow-Cooker Spanish Beef

INGREDIENTS

1 3-pound round, chuck or boneless pot roast

2 tablespoons olive oil

2 tablespoon butter

1 large Spanish onion; cut into thin rings.

2 cloves garlic

1/4 cup dry red cooking wine

2 14.5-oz. cans diced tomatoes

1/4 cup beef broth

1 bay leaf

1/2 teaspoon thyme

1/2 cup pimento-stuffed green olives

I love this Spanish version of a beef stew. It has great a great flavor and makes wonderful leftovers. Try this one in a slow cooker as I do on HSN!

PREPARATION:

Heat olive oil and butter in large heavy skillet over medium heat. Lightly brown the meat on all sides. Place roast into your Slow Cooker; keep skillet heating on stove.

Add the onion and garlic to the pan and cook for about 3 minutes. Add the wine quickly; scraping the bottom of the skillet. Add the tomatoes, beef broth, thyme and bay leaf; bring mixture to a boil. Pour tomato mixture over meat

Cook on Low for 6–7 hours adding the olives during the final hour of cooking.

Serve with rice.

Rotisserie Rack of Lamb

INGREDIENTS

1 4-pound rack of lamb; more or less depending on the size of your oven

Marinade
1/2 cup balsamic vinegar
1/3 cup Dijon or stone ground mustard
5 cloves garlic
1/4 cup fresh rosemary leaves
4 sprigs of fresh thyme
2 teaspoons salt
1 teaspoon coarse ground black pepper
2 Tablespoons extra virgin olive oil

This delicious dinner is easy to make when you use your rotisserie; however you can roast it in the oven if you do not have one! Try to let the meat marinate overnight or for 8 - 12 hours to get the best flavor!

PREPARATION

Place all of the marinade ingredients into your food processor or maxi-blend and process until smooth.

Wash and pat dry the lamb. Rub the marinade into the meat. Place the meat and the remaining marinade into a zip-top plastic bag. Squeeze as much air out of the bag as you can, seal and store in the refrigerator. If possible, turn the bag every now and then to redistribute marinade.

Remove the lamb from the refrigerator. Use tongs and remove lamb from bag; reserve any leftover marinade. Load onto your rotisserie spit; be careful not to touch any of the bones. Place spit in the oven with the drip pan underneath. Add 1/2 cup water to drip pan.

Roast for 15 – 18 minutes per pound or until the internal temperature reads 155° at the thickest part of the meat.

Remove from oven, cover loosely with aluminum foil and allow to rest before carving into chops.

FOR GRAVY

Melt 2 Tablespoons Butter in a small skillet. Add 2 teaspoons flour, the reserved marinade and drippings from oven. Heat to a boil and cook down for 5 minutes. Reduce heat and simmer until meat is carved. Just before serving stir in 2-3 tablespoons milk or cream.

Lamb Chops with Mint Pesto

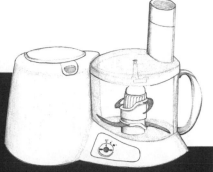

This dish is so good, there won't be any leftovers!

MINT PESTO:

Place the mint, parsley, walnuts and garlic into your food processor and pulse 1-2 times. With the machine on, slowly pour in 1 cup of the olive oil and continue to process until mixture is very finely chopped but not pureed. Pour the mixture into a glass bowl and season with the vinegar, 3/4 teaspoon salt and 1/4 teaspoon pepper. Set the mint pesto aside.

LAMB CHOPS:

Preheat the broiler in your convection oven to 400°.

Trim the excess fat from the chops and rub with the remaining olive oil. Sprinkle with the remaining salt and pepper.

Lightly spray or grease the broiler rack that came with your oven and arrange chops on top. Place the rack into the oven at mid-height and crack the door.

Broil the chops 4 minutes. Turn and cook another 2 minutes for medium rare, or until cooked to desired doneness. Arrange the chops onto serving plates and top with room temperature mint pesto.

SERVING SUGGESTION:

This is great with garlic mashed potatoes!

INGREDIENTS

1 cup packed fresh mint leaves

1/2 cup fresh parsley leaves

1/4 cup walnuts

3 cloves garlic

1 cup plus 2 tablespoons extra-virgin olive oil

2 tablespoons white wine vinegar

1 3/4 teaspoons salt

1/2 teaspoon pepper

8 lamb shoulder chops; about 7 ounces each

Rolled Leg of Lamb & Gyro Leftovers

INGREDIENTS

1 3-pound boneless rolled leg of lamb

Marinade
2 Tablespoons lemon juice
1 teaspoon lemon pepper
1/2 cup extra virgin olive oil
6 cloves garlic; minced
2 teaspoons dried rosemary leaves
1 teaspoon dried parsley
1 teaspoon dried thyme
1 1/2 teaspoons salt
1/2 teaspoon coarse ground pepper

I'm not sure which I like better, the lamb for dinner or the Gyros the next day. If you are having a get-together, just do the whole thing as Gyros! Be sure to serve with the Yogurt-Cucumber Sauce (recipe next page)!

PREPARATION:

Mix all marinade ingredients together in your Maxi-Blend, your food processor or using your immersion blender. Pour into a jumbo zip-top bag.

Untie the rolled lamb and place into bag with marinade. Squeeze out as much air as you can and seal the bag. Place the lamb in the refrigerator and let marinate 6-10 hours. Remove roast from bag, re-roll and tie securely.

Preheat your convection oven to 400°.

Place the roast on the spit of your rotisserie or onto a meat rack in a drip pan. Cook at 400° for 13-15 minutes per pound for medium or until an internal temperature, at the thickest part of the meat, reaches 155°.

Remove from oven, cover loosely with aluminum foil, and let rest 8-10 minutes before carving.

Gyros with Tzatziki

INGREDIENTS

1 pound cooked rolled leg of lamb; warm

2 large pita pocket breads

Shredded lettuce

Diced tomatoes

Yogurt- Cucumber Sauce

Yogurt- Cucumber Sauce:

3 cups plain yogurt

1 medium lemon; juiced

1/2 teaspoon garlic powder

1 cup cucumber; skinned, seeded and finely diced

1 Tablespoon + 2 teaspoons finely chopped fresh mint

Kosher salt and fresh ground black pepper to taste.

Cook a fresh Rolled Leg of Lamb as described on the preceding page, or use the leftovers!

PREPARATION:

Thinly slice the lamb and cut into bite-sized pieces.

Cut the pits breads in half so you have 4 half-circles. Put 1/4 of the lamb into each pita pocket. Add shredded lettuce and chopped tomatoes. Generously drizzle to top with the Yogurt-Cucumber Sauce.

Serve immediately!

YOGURT-CUCUMBER SAUCE (TZATZIKI):

My good friend Georgia coached me on this recipe. She taught me that careful draining prevents Gyros that drip down to your elbows! So enjoy—relatively drip-free!

Place the yogurt into a paper coffee filter or paper towel-lined colander. Let the yogurt drain for 1 hour, stirring every 15 minutes.

Place the prepared cucumber between paper towels and press out all the moisture; you may have to change paper towels and re-press 3 or 4 times.

After the yogurt and cucumber are well drained, mix together with the remaining ingredients. Store in the refrigerator, in an air-tight container, for at least 2 hours before using. May be kept for up to 4 days.

BBQ Chicken Sandwiches

FOOD PROCESSOR

INGREDIENTS

1 lb. boneless, skinless chicken breasts; split

3 cups water

2 Tablespoons granulated chicken bouillon

1 cup barbeque sauce

4 sandwich buns

Sliced onion, dill pickle chips, extra sauce (optional)

You can make this recipe in the Quad-Blade Processor or your Maxi-Blend! They are fast, easy and delicious!

PREPARATION:

Bring the water and bouillon to a boil in a medium saucepan. Add the chicken, reduce heat, and simmer covered 20-30 minutes.

FOR QUAD-BLADE PROCESSOR:

Using tongs, remove the chicken from the pan and place, hot, vertically into the Quad-Blade Processor around the blades.

Pulse three times. Remove lid and add barbeque sauce. Replace lid and pulse until sauce is evenly distributed and the meat is a finely chopped as you like.

FOR MAXI-BLEND:

Using tongs, remove half of the chicken from the pan and place, hot, vertically into the Maxi-Blend around the blades.

Pulse three times. Remove lid and add half of the barbeque sauce. Replace lid and pulse until sauce is evenly distributed and the meat is a finely chopped as you like.

Repeat with remaining chicken and sauce.

Split the sandwich buns and place 1/4 of the chicken on each bun. Add sliced onion, dill pickle chips and extra sauce if desired.

64

Chicken Chimichangas

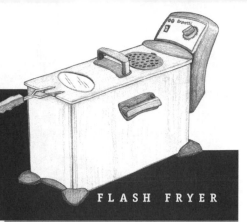

These delicious pockets remind me of when I lived in Texas! The combination of the warm soft middle surrounded by the crispy tortillas just can't be beat!

PREPARATION:

Combine the chicken, bouillon, cloves, bay leaves, celery ribs, garlic, salt and water in a large stockpot. Cook over medium heat 1 – 1 1/2 hours or until chicken is tender. Remove from heat and let stand until cooled. Remove chicken from liquid and chop.

Sauté minced garlic, onion and olive oil in a skillet, over medium heat, until onions are tender. Add the chicken, pimentos, chopped chilies, cumin, chili powder, salt and pepper to taste. Simmer over low heat for 10 – 15 minutes. Remove from heat and stir in 1 cup shredded Cheddar and 1 cup shredded Monterey Jack cheese.

Preheat Flash Fryer to 375°. Heat a skillet with 2 inches water until boiling.

To assemble, make one at a time in the following manner:

Use tongs and lower a tortilla into water and quickly turn it over and then remove to a work surface; tortilla should only be in water for 10 seconds!

Spread about 1/2 cup chicken mixture horizontally across middle of tortilla leaving about 1 1/2 - 2 inches on each side. Fold the bottom of the tortilla up, fold in the sides and roll it tightly. Place, folded side down on a non-stick surface.

Repeat this procedure for the remaining tortillas and filling.

Using a large slotted spoon, carefully lower the filled tortillas into the lowered basket of your fryer. Do not over crowd! You may be only able to fry 2 or 3 at a time!

Fry 3 – 4 minutes or until tortilla is light brown and crispy. Drain on paper towels.

TO SERVE:

Remove toothpicks and place 1 or 2 Chimichangas on a plate.   Top each with 1/4 cup shredded cheese, 1/4 cup sour cream and 2 Tablespoons guacamole. Surround with shredded lettuce and chopped tomato. Serve immediately!

Have a bowl of fresh Salsa on the table to pass around if desired.

PARTY TIP:

Make these ahead using the small soft taco tortillas and reheat in your convection oven. Arrange on a platter strewn with shredded lettuce. Have bowls of the sour cream, guacamole, salsa and cheese nearby.

Serve with Margaritas or Sangria!

INGREDIENTS

3 lbs. boneless, skinless chicken breasts

3 Tablespoons chicken bouillon granules

2 cloves

2 bay leaves

2 celery ribs

2 large garlic cloves

1 teaspoon salt

5 cups water

1 large onion; thinly sliced

1 clove garlic; minced

2 Tablespoons Olive Oil

14-oz. Jar chopped pimento; drained

1 10-ounce can Rotel; drained

1 4.5-ounce can diced green chilies

1/2 teaspoon cumin

1/4 teaspoon chili powder

1 cup shredded Cheddar Cheese

1 cup shredded Monterey Jack Cheese

Salt and pepper to taste

8 large flour tortillas

2 cups sour cream (optional)

1 cup guacamole (optional)

2 cups shredded Cheddar cheese (optional)

Shredded lettuce (optional)

1 large tomato; chopped (optional)

Fresh Salsa (optional)

Southern Deep-Fried Chicken

INGREDIENTS

3 lbs. Chicken pieces; bone-in

8 cups cool water

2 Tablespoons salt

1 1/2 cups flour

2 teaspoons salt

1 teaspoon paprika

1/2 teaspoon ground black pepper

I was never able to make good fried chicken until I started using the Bravetti Flash Fryer. Now I make it on HSN when I demonstrate the fryer because it comes out perfectly every single time! it's not fancy, but it sure is good—hot or cold! Just ask my son, Max, he adores it and I get a lot of pleasure from his enjoyment!

PREPARATION:

Wash chicken and place into 8 cups water with 2 Tablespoons salt. Allow to soak for 30 minutes. Drain water and pat chicken dry.

Preheat your Deep Fryer to 375°.

Place flour and seasonings into a large zip-close baggie. Add chicken, 2-3 pieces at a time, to baggie and toss to thoroughly coat chicken pieces. Allow to sit 5 minutes and then toss again.

When fryer temperature indicator light goes out, remove lid and lower basket. Using long tongs, gently place chicken, one piece at a time, into the oil. Do not overcrowd the fryer. You may have to cook the chicken in two batches.

Cover fryer and cook for 13-15 minutes or until done. Raise lid and allow draining 30 seconds. Place chicken onto paper towel to remove any excess oils. Repeat with remaining chicken.

HINT: If you will be cooking several batches of chicken, place the cooked chicken in an oven-safe dish and keep warm, uncovered, and in a 225 ∫ oven until all chicken is ready to serve.

66

Supper Time! Entrées for All! **ELECTRIC EATS** E

Rotisserie Chicken

Nothing makes your mouth water like the smell of a chicken cooking on your rotisserie. No matter what seasonings you use, everybody will be ready for dinner!

PREPARATION:

Remove the insides of the chicken and discard. Wash the chicken thoroughly and pat dry. Use you kitchen shears and trim the neck and tail to be flush with the cavity opening.

Skewer the chicken lengthwise with your rotisserie spit, evenly distributing the weight. Pull the legs up and together and tie them in place using the kitchen twine. Secure the wings by tucking them under or tying them.

Do a trial run by place the chicken into the oven and turn the rotisserie on just long enough to make sure the chicken will not hit the top elements or the drip pan underneath! Remove chicken.

Time to Season! Pour the oil into your hands and massage the surface of the chicken with it. Sprinkle the chicken with the rub of your choice and massage into the oil.

Return chicken to oven and turn thermostat to 450° and turn rotisserie feature on. Cook 15 minutes. Reduce heat to 375° and continue cooking until internal temperature of the thickest part of the thigh reaches 175°; about 15-20 minutes per pound total cooking time.

INGREDIENTS

1 – 3 1/2 - 4 pound chicken (buy according to the size of your rotisserie)

Rotisserie Rub of your choice (see recipe index)

Kitchen twine

2 Tablespoons Vegetable or Olive Oil

Meat thermometer

Meat Rubs

To make these rubs, simply combine all ingredients in a small mixing bowl. Stir with a fork to blend. You may store these in an airtight container for up to 6 months so I suggest that when you find the one you love, buy the seasonings in bulk and double or triple the recipe for future use!

Never-Fail Rotisserie Rub
2 tablespoons firmly packed light brown sugar
1 tablespoon garlic salt
1 tablespoon onion salt
1 teaspoon celery salt
1/3 cup paprika
1 tablespoon coarse ground black pepper

Barbeque Rub
1/4 cup kosher salt
1/4 cup paprika
1/3 cup firmly packed light brown sugar
1 teaspoon garlic powder
1 teaspoon onion powder
2 teaspoons celery salt

Mediterranean Rub
2 Tablespoons dried oregano leaves
2 Tablespoons dried rosemary
1/2 cup dried thyme leaves
1/4 cup dried basil leaves
3 Tablespoons kosher salt
2 teaspoons coarse ground black pepper
3 Tablespoons dried lemon peel

Ranch Rub
3 tablespoons dried parsley
1 1/2 teaspoons dried oregano
1 1/2 teaspoons dried tarragon
2 teaspoons garlic salt
2 teaspoons lemon pepper
1 Tablespoon dried chives

Caribbean Jerk Rub
1 teaspoon ground nutmeg
1 teaspoon ground cinnamon
2 teaspoons dried thyme
2 teaspoons ground allspice
2 teaspoons ground black pepper
1 teaspoon cayenne pepper
2 Tablespoons onion salt
2 teaspoons sugar
2 teaspoons garlic salt

Home Style Seasoned Salt
3/4 cup kosher salt
1/4 cup garlic salt
1 1/2 teaspoons coarse ground black pepper
1 teaspoon dried oregano leaves
2 teaspoons paprika
2 teaspoons celery salt
1/2 teaspoon stone ground mustard

68

Supper Time! Entrées for All!   ELECTRIC EATS   E

Lemon Chicken Bake

This is an easy good-anytime recipe that everyone seems to like!

PREPARATION:

Preheat your convection oven to 375°.

Grease with shortening a shallow, oven-safe dish large enough to accommodate the chicken pieces without touching each other and that will fit into your oven.

Wash the chicken well and pat dry.

Mix together the bread crumbs and all the spices and put onto a plate.

Beat the egg with the water in a shallow bowl.

Dip the chicken, one piece at a time, into the egg wash and then press into the bread crumb mixture, covering well. Repeat with remaining chicken.

Place the chicken into the dish. Cover with foil and bake 30 minutes. Remove foil and place one or two slices of lemon on each piece of chicken. Continue baking another 15 – 20 minutes or until golden brown and crispy on the out side.

INGREDIENTS

4 boneless, skinless chicken breast halves

1 cup plain dried bread crumbs

1 Tablespoon dried lemon peel

1 teaspoon coarse ground black pepper

1 teaspoon dried thyme leaves

1/2 teaspoon onion salt

1 teaspoon garlic salt

2 Tablespoons dried parsley flakes

1 egg

3 Tablespoons water

1 lemon; thinly sliced

Shortening

Chicken Cordon Bleu

INGREDIENTS

4 skinless, boneless chicken breast halves

1/2 teaspoon salt

1/4 teaspoon ground white or black pepper

6 slices Swiss cheese

4 sliced cooked ham

1 cup seasoned bread crumbs

This is much easier to make than you may think and incredibly good!

PREPARATION:

Preheat convection oven to 350°.

Spray an 8x8-inch or 9x9-inch baking dish with nonstick cooking spray.

Place chicken breasts on waxed paper and pound to 1/4 inch thickness.

Sprinkle each piece of chicken on both sides with the salt and pepper. Place 1 slice cheese and 1 slice ham on each breast. Roll up each breast and secure with a wooden toothpick.

Place the bread crumbs on a plate. Roll each piece of chicken in the bread crumbs until lightly coated on all sides. Place into baking dish.

Bake for 30 to 35 minutes, or until the chicken is no longer pink. Remove from oven and place 1/2 slice of cheese on each piece of chicken. Return to oven and bake another 3 to 5 minutes or until the cheese has melted.

Remove toothpicks and serve immediately.

70

Supper Time! Entrées for All! ELECTRIC EATS E

Chicken & Biscuit Bake

Always a family favorite!

PREPARATION:

Preheat convection oven to 350°. Lightly grease a 9x13-inch baking dish (use a deep 9x9 if a 9x13 won't fit into your oven).

In a medium skillet, melt butter over medium heat. Add onion and sauté until tender. Turn the heat up to medium-high. Add garlic and cook about a minute just to release the flavor.

Stir in the flour, sugar, salt, basil and pepper to make a paste. Slowly add the chicken broth, stirring constantly, until mixture reaches a boil. Boil for 1 minute continuing to stir and scrape the bottom of the pan. Reduce heat and stir in vegetables. Simmer 5 minutes and add chicken. Pour mixture into the prepared baking dish.

Combine biscuit mix and basil. Add the milk and mix to form a dough ball. Divide the dough into 6 to 8 even-sized balls. Flatten the balls to equal thickness and place on top of the chicken mixture.

Bake uncovered for 30 minutes. Cover with foil to prevent biscuits from over-browning and continue cooking another 10 minutes.

To serve, remove the biscuits to individual serving plates and ladle the chicken mixture over top.

INGREDIENTS

1/4 cup butter

2 cloves garlic; minced

1/2 cup chopped onion

1/2 cup flour

2 teaspoons sugar

1 teaspoon salt

1 teaspoon dried basil

1/2 teaspoon ground black pepper

4 cups chicken broth

1 1-pound bag frozen mixed veggies; thawed

4 cups diced cooked chicken

2 cups buttermilk biscuit mix

2 teaspoons dried basil

2/3 cup milk

E ELECTRIC EATS   Supper Time! Entrées for All!

71

Caramelized Chicken

INGREDIENTS

1 3-pound whole cut-up chicken or your favorite chicken pieces

2 Tablespoons olive oil

1/2 cup soy sauce

2 Tablespoons ketchup

1 cup honey

1 clove garlic; minced

1/2 teaspoon cayenne pepper

This sticky, sweet 'n tangy chicken is finger-licking good! Be sure to have plenty of napkins handy!

PREPARATION:

Preheat convection oven to 375°.

Wash and pat dry the chicken pieces. Place into a thoroughly greased baking dish.

Mix together all remaining ingredients. Pour over chicken.

Bake, uncovered, for one hour or until sauce is caramelized.

72

Supper Time! Entrées for All!   ELECTRIC EATS E

Make-Ahead Honey Curried Chicken

This delicious dish can be prepared ahead of time and refrigerated until you are ready to bake it. Add extra curry powder for a hotter dish!

PREPARATION:

Wash and pat dry the chicken breasts. Arrange them in a greased 8x8-inch baking dish.

In a measuring cup, combine the butter, honey, mustard, curry powder, cayenne pepper and salt. Mix together with a fork until well blended and creamy. Pour over chicken. Cover and refrigerate until ready to bake.

Preheat convection oven to 375°.

Bake the chicken, uncovered, for 20 minutes basting once. Turn chicken over and baste again. Bake and additional 20 minutes, or until chicken is tender, basting one more time.

Serve with hot white rice.

INGREDIENTS

4 boneless, skinless chicken breast halves

1/4 cup butter; melted

1/4 cup honey

3 heaping Tablespoons Dijon style mustard

2 teaspoons curry powder

Pinch cayenne pepper

1/4 teaspoon salt

Forty-Clove Chicken

INGREDIENTS

1 3-pound frying chicken; cut into serving size pieces

1/4 teaspoon salt

1/4 teaspoon paprika

40 cloves garlic (about 2 heads)

3 Tablespoons lemon juice

1 Tablespoon dried lemon zest

1/2 cup dry white wine

1/4 cup vermouth

1/4 cup olive oil

2 Tablespoons freshly chopped parsley

2 teaspoons dried basil leaves

1 teaspoon dried oregano leaves

Pinch red pepper flakes

6 green onions; whites and light green parts thinly sliced

I have tried many versions of this recipe throughout the years, but none of them tasted quite right! I hope you like my rendition!

PREPARATION:

Preheat convection oven to 375°.

Wash and pat dry the chicken. Arrange the chicken, skin side up, in a single layer on a shallow baking pan. Sprinkle with the salt and paprika and rub into the skin. Sprinkle the parsley, basil and oregano over the top.

Peel garlic and put into a small mixing bowl.

Add to the garlic the lemon juice, lemon zest, wine, vermouth, olive oil, parsley, basil, oregano, red pepper flakes and sliced onion together in a small bow; mix well. Drizzle the mixture evenly over the chicken.

Cover with foil and bake 40 minutes. Uncover and bake an additional 15 minutes or until chicken is done.

Chicken-Asparagus Casserole

This warm and hearty casserole is very good and something a little different to take along to pot lucks!

PREPARATION:

Preheat oven to 350°. Grease 9x13-inch baking dish.

Heat oil in medium skillet and sauté the peppers, onions and garlic until veggies are cooked but still crisp.

Mix soup, eggs, ricotta cheese and 1 cup cheddar cheese until well blended. Add the onion mixture, chicken, asparagus and noodles; mix well.

Spread mixture into pan and top with remaining cheddar cheese.

Bake, uncovered, 30 minutes or until center is set and cheese is bubbly.

INGREDIENTS

2 teaspoons vegetable oil

1 cup red bell pepper; seeds and membrane removed, chopped fine

1 medium onion; finely chopped

2 cloves garlic; minced

1 10.75-ounce can condensed cream of asparagus soup

2 eggs

8 ounces ricotta cheese

2 cups shredded cheddar cheese; divided

1 1/2 cups cooked chicken; chopped

10-ounce package frozen asparagus; thawed and drained

8 ounces egg noodles; cooked

Slow-Cooker Chicken

INGREDIENTS

1 3-4 pound whole chicken
1/4 cup meat rub of your choice
2 Tablespoons softened butter
1 18-inch piece aluminum foil

Cooking a chicken in your slow cooker is a great way to come home to a hot meal, even if you are very limited in time in the morning. Choose one of the meat rubs listed in the index and make it ahead. Then, in the morning you are all set!

PREPARATION:

Fold the aluminum foil over three times length-wise. Place across the middle of the slow cooker (width-wise) to form a sling with which to remove your chicken.

Wash and pat dry the chicken. Use your hands and rub the butter all over the skin of the chicken. Sprinkle the seasoning rub all over the chicken.

Place the chicken into the slow cooker. Place on the lid.

Cook 6-7 hours on low or 4-5 hours on high heat.

Remove the chicken to a platter and cover loosely with aluminum foil to keep warm before carving.

You can strain the fat from the liquid in the slow cooker and make gravy on your stove top if desired.

76

Supper Time! Entrées for All! ELECTRIC EATS E

Rotisserie Game Hens

When you are looking for something "different" for dinner, try game hen! They are easy, delicious and not very expensive. Try using any of the meat rubs listed in the index under "rubs", or try the Hoi sin Style on the next page.   No matter what the mood your palette is in, game hen will hit the spot!

INGREDIENTS

2 Cornish Game Hens

1/2 cup meat rub of your choice OR simply salt and pepper

Kitchen twine

Meat thermometer

PREPARATION:

Wash and pat dry the game hen.

Load the birds onto the rotisserie spit, legs toward each other. Turn the birds so that one is upside down and the cavities are touching. Use kitchen twine and tie the legs and, if necessary, the wings, so that nothing "flops around" during cooking.

Load the spit into the rotisserie and turn oven temperature to 400° and rotisserie on. Roast until the thickest part of the thigh reaches 175° on a meat thermometer (about 45-60 minutes).

Remove from oven and cover loosely with aluminum foil. Allow to sit until spit is cool enough to handle.

Remove hens from spit, cut away twine and cut each hen in half, slicing through the breast bone. Serve immediately.

If you do not have a rotisserie: You can roast the hens in the oven at 375° following the same temperature guidelines.

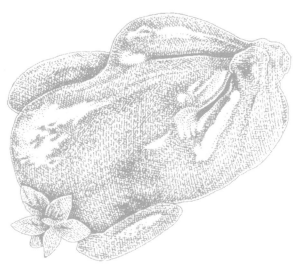

E ELECTRIC EATS   Supper Time! Entrées for All!

77

Hoi sin-Style Game Hen

INGREDIENTS

1 Tablespoons olive oil

1 Tablespoon Chinese five-spice powder

2 Cornish Game Hens

1/3 cup Hoi sin Sauce

1 Tablespoon rice vinegar

1 Tablespoon toasted sesame oil

1 Tablespoon toasted sesame seeds

2 green onions; white and light green parts sliced thin

Sweet and spicy, these game hen will fill the house with a wonderful aroma! They also look beautiful when plated so consider serving them at a get-together.

PREPARATION:

Wash and pat dry the game hen.

In a small bowl, make a paste of the oil and five-spice powder. Rub the paste over each game hen. Place the hens into a large zip bag and refrigerate for 2 hours or over night.

In another bowl, combine the Hoi sin sauce, vinegar and sesame oil. Cover and refrigerate until ready to cook the birds.

Remove the hens from the bag and pat dry. Load the birds onto the rotisserie spit, legs toward each other. Turn the birds so that one is upside down and the cavities are touching. Use kitchen twine and tie the legs and, if necessary, the wings, so that nothing "flops around" during cooking.

Load the spit into the rotisserie and turn oven temperature to 400° and rotisserie on. Roast until the thickest part of the thigh reaches 175° on a meat thermometer (about 45-60 minutes).   During last 15 minutes of cooking, baste the hens 2-3 times with the Hoi sin mixture. Remove from oven and cover loosely with aluminum foil. Allow to sit until spit is cool enough to handle.

Remove hens from spit, cut away twine and cut each hen in half, slicing through the breast bone. Arrange on a bed of white rice and sprinkle with toasted sesame seeds and green onion slices.

78

Supper Time! Entrées for All!   ELECTRIC EATS   E

Tangy Broiled Pork Chops

This is an easy, quick but delicious dinner! It's great with rice or mashed potatoes and a green salad.

PREPARATION:

Heat together in a medium, non-reactive, saucepan the ketchup, water, vinegar, Worcestershire sauce, brown sugar, honey, onion salt, salt and chili powder. Bring to a boil. Reduce heat to low and simmer 5 minutes. Remove from heat. Pour half of the sauce into a small bowl for later.

Preheat your Broiler on 400°.

Wash and pat dry the pork chops. Brush both sides of the chops with the sauce and place onto the broiler rack. Place the pan in the center of your oven (about 4-5 inches from the heat) and broil for 4 minutes. Remember to leave the door cracked!

Remove the pan and brush with more sauce. Turn chops and brush the other side; broil another 4 minutes. Continue turning and basting every 4 minutes until chops are done and juices run clear.

Serve with remaining sauce.

INGREDIENTS

3/4 cup ketchup

3/4 cup water

3 Tablespoons white vinegar

1 Tablespoon Worcestershire Sauce

1 Tablespoon firmly packed brown sugar

1 Tablespoon Honey

1/2 teaspoon onion salt

1/2 teaspoon salt

1/2 teaspoon chili powder

6 (3/4-inch) thick boneless pork chops

CONVECTION OVEN

Glazed Roasted Pork Loin

INGREDIENTS

1 4-pound boneless pork loin; rolled and tied

1 Tablespoon Dijon mustard

1 teaspoon kosher salt

1 teaspoon coarse ground black pepper

Marinade/Glaze:

1/2 cup port wine or sherry

2 Tablespoons soy sauce

2 cloves garlic; crushed

1/4 cup red currant jelly

1 teaspoon vegetable oil

This roast is easy to prepare but is elegant enough for guests or a special family dinner! It needs to marinate for about two hours, so plan accordingly. If you like, make the gravy below to serve with this meat!

PREPARATION:

Wash and pat dry the pork roast. In a small bowl, combine the mustard, salt and pepper; rub mixture all over the roast. Place roast into a large zip-top bag. In a measuring cup, mix together the wine, soy sauce and garlic; pour into the bag with the meat. Remove as much air as you can from the bag and seal. Place into the refrigerator for 2-3 hours.

Preheat Convection Oven to 325°.

Remove meat from bag, reserving marinade, and place roast into a shallow roasting pan. Roast pork, uncovered, for about 2 hours or until meat thermometer reads 170° at the thickest part of the meat.

While the meat is roasting, combine in a small saucepan, 2 Tablespoons of the reserved marinade with the red currant jelly and the oil. Cook over medium heat just until the jelly has melted. Brush onto the meat 3 to 4 times during the last 30 minutes of roasting. Remove roast from oven, cover loosely with aluminum foil and allow meat to rest 10 minutes before carving into thin slices.

FOR GRAVY:

Remove any excess oil from pan and discard. Place the pan over heat and scrape up any bits. Bring to a boil and add remaining reserved marinade. Allow to cook down until meat has been sliced. Serve with the thinly sliced pork.

80

Southern-Fried Pork Chops

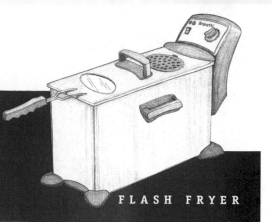

INGREDIENTS

6 thin cut, bone-in pork chops (about 1- 1 1/2 pounds)

1 1/2 cups flour

1 teaspoon salt

1 teaspoon coarse ground black pepper

Oil for frying

Always a favorite in my family! I think these turn out best in the flash fryer, but you can pan fry them in a thin layer of vegetable oil if you prefer! I serve these with rice, tomato gravy and home made biscuits when I'm feeling very Southern!

PREPARATION:

Pre-heat your Flash Fryer to 375°. Insert and lower the basket.

Wash and pat dry the pork chops.

Place the flour, salt and pepper into a large zip-top bag and toss until mixed.

Place the pork chops into the bag and toss until well coated. Remove from bag and place, in a single layer on a plate. Let them sit 10 minutes or until fryer is preheated.

Working with one chop at a time, put back in baggie and re-toss in the flour. Using long tongs remove the chop from the baggie and shake off any excess flour. Drop directly into the fryer.

Repeat with remaining chops but, do not over crowd the fryer; you may only be able to fry 3 at a time depending on the size of your fryer.

Fry for 4-5 minutes or until golden brown.

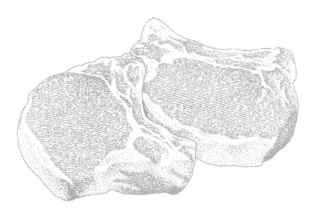

Sweet and Sour Pineapple Pork

INGREDIENTS

1 pound lean boneless pork; washed and cut into 1-inch cubes

Cornstarch for coating

4-6 cups hot fluffy white rice

Batter Mix:

3/4 cup flour

1/4 cup cornstarch

1/2 teaspoon sugar

3/4 cup water

1 1/4 teaspoons baking powder

1/2 teaspoon vegetable oil

Sweet and Sour Pineapple Sauce:

1/2 teaspoon oil

2 cloves garlic; minced

1/4 cup cold water

2 Tablespoons cornstarch

1/2 cup white vinegar

1/2 cup packed brown sugar

3 Tablespoons ketchup

2 1/2 teaspoons soy sauce

Dash Tabasco (optional)

1 medium onion; very coarsely chopped

1 medium green bell pepper; seeds removed and very coarsely chopped

1 14-ounce can pineapple chunks; drained but reserving liquid

This is just like the Chinese make but you don't have to go get it! Try serving with Veggie Spring Rolls and hot fluffy white rice.

PREPARATION:

Preheat your Flash Fryer to 375°. Insert and lower basket.

Prepare pork cubes and place into a zip-top bag. Add enough cornstarch to coat pork. Set aside.

Make the batter; set aside.

In a measuring cup, whisk the cornstarch into the cold water until dissolved. Mix in the reserved pineapple juice, vinegar, brown sugar, ketchup, soy sauce and Tabasco sauce; set aside.

In a medium skillet, heat the oil over medium-high heat. Add the garlic, onion and green pepper. sauté quickly, stirring constantly 2 to 3 minutes or until vegetables are crisp-tender. Add the pineapple chunks and cook until just heated.

Pour in the liquid mixture. Bring to a boil. Reduce heat and simmer on low heat 5 to 10 minutes or until mixture is beginning to thicken and pork is ready.

Remove the cornstarch-coated pork cubes from the bag. Dip into the batter and immediately place, one cube at a time, into the hot fryer. Fry pork 4 to 5 minutes or until golden brown. Raise the basket and allow the pork to drain.

You now have two options; either way is fine!

1) Place the pork onto the hot rice and ladle sauce over top, or
2) Put the pork into the sauce, stir gently and ladle pork and sauce over he hot rice.

Stuffed Pork Roll-Ups and Sauerkraut

CONVECTION OVEN

I just love this dish! You can omit the sauerkraut if you want to, but I think it makes a great accompaniment!

PREPARATION:

Preheat convection oven to 350°.

Wash, pat dry and prepare the pork steaks as directed above. Pound the steaks to a 1/4-inch even thickness. Sprinkle both sides with salt and pepper. Lay flat on a sheet of waxed paper.

Tear the bread into small pieces and place into a small bowl; you should have about 2 cups. Add the raisins, celery, apple, salt and sage. Toss until mixed. Spread the mixture evenly across the steaks.

Roll the steaks and secure with wooden toothpicks.

Heat a thin layer of oil in a large skillet over medium-high heat.

Dust each roll-up with flour and place into the hot oil. Brown the meat on all sides. Remove from oil and place directly into a baking dish.

Bake, uncovered, for 1 hour. Serve on hot sauerkraut.

INGREDIENTS

6 pork steaks; bone removed and fat trimmed

Salt and pepper to taste

2-3 slices day-old bread

1/4 cup raisins

1/2 cup celery; chopped

1/4 cup apple; chopped

1/2 teaspoon salt

1 teaspoon sage

Flour

Oil for browning

1 can sauerkraut; drained and warmed

E ELECTRIC EATS   Supper Time! Entrées for All!

83

Pork Chops and Olives

INGREDIENTS

6 boneless pork chops

1 teaspoon coarse ground black pepper

2 Tablespoons Olive Oil

1 medium onion; chopped

2 cloves garlic; minced

1 28-ounce can diced tomatoes

1 cup small pimento-stuffed green olives

Hot fluffy white rice.

I really like this dish! I just sort of made it up one night using different ingredients I had available in my kitchen and I was surprised by how good it came out. Serve with white rice.

PREPARATION:

Preheat convection oven to 325°.

Wash and pat dry the pork chops. Sprinkle both sides with the pepper.

Heat the olive oil in a medium skillet over medium-high heat. Sear the pork chops 2-3 minutes on each side or until browned.

Reduce heat to medium. Remove the chops from the pan and place into a baking dish.

Add the onion and garlic and quick sauté, stirring constantly, 2-3 minutes or until onion is tender-crisp. Pour in the tomatoes and olives and heat through.

Pour the tomato mixture over the pork chops.

Cover with aluminum foil and bake 30 minutes. Remove foil and bake an additional 30 minutes.

Serve over white rice.

Old-Fashioned Stuffed Pork Chops

This is just the ticket for a hearty family meal or a dinner party with friends! The cranberry sauce adds just the sweetness it needs!

PREPARATION:

Wash and pat dry the pork chops. Using a very sharp, thin knife cut a pocket into the side of each chop about 3 inches long and 2 inches deep. Lightly salt and pepper both sides of the chops and set aside.

Make the stuffing and let cool.

OLD-FASHIONED BREAD STUFFING:

Tear the bread into small pieces or cubes; you should have 3 cups.

In a medium sauce pan, melt the butter over medium-low heat. Add the celery and onion and cook until vegetables are soft; about 6 minutes. Remove from heat

Add the bread, thyme and sage; toss gently to combine. Add the chicken broth, a little at a time, until the stuffing holds together. The amount used will depend on how dry the bread was. Allow stuffing to cool.

PREPARATION:

Preheat convection oven to 325°. Generously grease a baking dish with shortening.

Stuff each chop with about 1/4 cup stuffing. It is not necessary to close the opening so fill it to capacity so the cut edge gapes open. Place stuffed chops into prepared baking dish stuffing side facing the center of the pan.

Cover pan with aluminum foil. Bake, on center rack, 45 minutes.

Remove pan from oven and uncover. Top each chop with a generous amount of the cranberry sauce.

Return pan to oven and bake an additional 15-20 minutes.

INGREDIENTS

6 center cut, 3/4-inch thick, boneless pork chops

Salt and pepper

Old-Fashioned Bread Stuffing

Whole-berry cranberry sauce

Shortening

Old-Fashioned Bread Stuffing

2 Tablespoons butter

1/2 cup onion; finely chopped

1 celery stalk; finely chopped

1 1/2 teaspoon dried thyme

1 teaspoon dried sage; crumbled

1/2 teaspoon salt

3 cups soft breadcrumbs (about 5-6 slices day-old white bread)

1/2 cup hot chicken broth

Apricot-Glazed Rotisserie Pork Roast

INGREDIENTS

1 3-pound pork loin roast

1 1/2 teaspoons salt

1/2 teaspoon coarse ground black pepper

2 cloves garlic

1 Tablespoon dried rosemary leaves

2 Tablespoons Dijon mustard

Apricot Glaze

1 cup apricot preserves

1 Tablespoon brown sugar

2 Tablespoons Dijon mustard

1 Tablespoon lemon juice

Pork roasts, no matter which seasonings you choose, turn out great in your rotisserie. Below is one of the tastiest ways, I believe, to season a pork roast, but experiment with the different meat rubs (see index) and choose your favorite!

PREPARATION:

Wash and pat dry the pork roast. Make a paste with the salt, pepper, garlic, rosemary and mustard. Set aside.

Skewer the roast on the spit. Use your hands and rub the mustard paste all over the roast. Fit the skewered roast into your oven and turn on to 375°. Roast for 40 minutes.

Baste the roast with the Apricot Glaze, every 5-8 minutes, until the roast is done. It should read 160° on your meat thermometer. Remove meat from the spit rod and baste one more time. Cover loosely with aluminum foil and let rest 10 minutes before carving.

APRICOT GLAZE:

Combine the glaze ingredients in a small sauce pan and heat over medium heat until preserves are melted. Reduce heat and simmer 15 minutes. Reduce heat to very low and keep warm.

Baste roast as directed above and serve remaining glaze with the carved meat.

Honey-Crusted Ham

This tastes very similar to that spiral-sliced ham so popular during the holidays. However, it costs much less! There are two methods of cooking this ham; oven or rotisserie. If your rotisserie is large enough, I encourage you to use it for this recipe. The rotisserie makes the glaze crusty all over. If you must use your oven, be sure to use a roasting rack.

PREPARATION:

Prepare the ham by loading on your rotisserie spit or onto a roasting rack.

If using your convection oven, preheat to 375°.

Eventually, you will cook the ham until a meat thermometer registers 160° at the thickest part of the ham; about 15 minutes per pound for rotisserie or 20 minutes per pound for convection oven. Be sure not to touch the bone with the thermometer when taking your reading.

While the ham is cooking, combine the ingredients for the glaze in a small bowl until smooth.

About 30 minutes before the ham is done, remove it from the oven.

Brush the glaze all over the ham and then sprinkle the raw sugar over the entire surface. Return to oven until the ham is done.

Remove the ham from the spit, being careful not to dislodge the crust. Cover loosely with aluminum foil and let rest for 10 minutes before slicing.

INGREDIENTS

1 5-pound fully-cooked bone-in or boneless ham

1/2 cup raw sugar crystals

Spiced Honey Glaze:

1/2 cup honey

2 teaspoons lemon juice

1 teaspoon ground cinnamon

1/8 teaspoon ground cloves

Potatoes and Ham Dinner

INGREDIENTS

5 pounds small red new potatoes; quartered

1/2 cup butter; softened

16-ounces sour cream

1 10.75-ounce can condensed cream of chicken soup

2 cups shredded sharp cheddar cheese

2 Tablespoons dried chives

2 cups cooked ham; chopped or cubed

1 teaspoon coarse ground black pepper

1 teaspoon salt

1 1/2 cup corn flakes; crushed

1/4 cup butter; melted

This delicious and filling dinner is a guaranteed family-pleaser! Plus, it's large enough for a pot-luck take-along dish!

PREPARATION:

Preheat convection oven to 325°. Generously grease a 9x13-inch pan with shortening.

Place potatoes into a large pot of rapidly boiling water. Cook until just tender; about 10-12 minutes. Drain and place in a large mixing bowl. Pour the melted butter over the potatoes and toss.

In a medium mixing bowl, combine the sour cream, soup, cheese, chives, ham, pepper and salt. Pour this mixture over the potatoes and butter; toss lightly.

Spread potato mixture into the prepared baking dish. Sprinkle with the corn flakes and drizzle on the butter.

Bake for 30 minutes.

Dijon Salmon Bake

CONVECTION OVEN

This is a great way to get your family to eat fish—because it's really good! Serve with hot buttered noodles or rice.

PREPARATION:

Preheat Convection Oven to 400°.

In a small bowl, mix together the butter, mustard and honey; set aside. In another bowl, combine the breadcrumbs, pecans and parsley.

Wash and pat dry the salmon. Lay the filets on a shallow baking pan. Lightly salt and pepper each fillet.

Brush the honey mustard mixture on each fillet and then sprinkle the bread crumb mixture on top.

Bake for 10 – 12 minutes or until the fish flakes easily with a fork.

Serve immediately with lemon wedges.

INGREDIENTS

4 salmon filets (4-ounces each); skin on the bottom

1/4 cup butter; melted

3 Tablespoons Dijon mustard

1 1/2 Tablespoons honey

1/4 cup dried plain breadcrumbs

1/4 cup pecans; finely chopped

4 teaspoons fresh parsley; finely chopped

Salt and pepper to taste

1 lemon cut into wedges

Baked Stuffed Shrimp

INGREDIENTS

1 pound large shrimp; shelled and deveined (about 12)

1 1/4 cup coarse fresh bread crumbs (about 2 slices bread)

4 Tablespoons butter

6-8 green onions; whites and light green parts thinly sliced (about 1 cup)

2 teaspoons garlic; minced

1/2 teaspoon paprika

4 Tablespoons fresh parsley; chopped

2 Tablespoons dried crushed basil leaves

1/2 teaspoon salt

1/2 teaspoon coarse ground black pepper

3 Tablespoon olive oil

3 Tablespoons parmesan cheese

1 lemon cut into wedges.

This dish takes a little time to prepare, but cooks in a snap! it's great for a dinner party because you can do all the prep work ahead and then bake just before serving. Try making these to serve along with a small grilled filet for your next cookout!

PREPARATION:

Preheat convection oven to 500°.

Tear the bread slices into very small pieces and lay them on a flat pan. Place them into the oven until they turn golden brown; stir as necessary.

Melt the butter in a saucepan and add the green onions and garlic. Cook until the vegetables are crisp-tender. Add the breadcrumbs, paprika, thyme, parsley, basil, salt and pepper; toss to blend.

Butterfly the shrimp by slicing 3/4 of the way through the underside of the shrimp lengthwise. Lay the shrimp, cut side up, flat on a pan. Spread an equal amount of stuffing on each shrimp, pressing the stuffing into the crevice and smoothing down the top.

If you are going to bake these later, cover securely with plastic wrap and refrigerate for up to 8 hours.

Before baking, brush each shrimp lightly with olive oil and top with a sprinkling of parmesan cheese. Place into your preheated oven and cook 6-8 minutes or until shrimp is pink and stuffing is beginning to brown.

Serve hot with lemon wedges.

Shrimp and Crab Quiche

I like this quiche served with a crisp Caesar salad and a glass of white wine; perfect for a light supper!

PREPARATION:

Preheat oven to 375°.

Unfold the pie crust and place into the bottom of a 9-inch pie or quiche pan. Press into the corners and crimp the upper edge with your fingers or a fork. Place a circular piece of parchment paper onto the bottom of the pie crust and weight down with dried beans or aluminum weight pellets. Place into the oven and bake 8 minutes. Remove from oven, discard paper and beans and let the crust cool.

Melt the butter in a small skillet and cook the onion and garlic for 2-3 minutes; do not let them brown. Add in the wine, dill, shrimp and crab. Cook, stirring, for about 2 minutes or until heated through. Remove from heat.

In a mixing bowl, whisk together the eggs, cream, milk, salt, pepper and 1/4 cup of the cheese. Stir in the seafood mixture.

Pour into partially baked pie crust and sprinkle with the remaining cheese.

Bake for about 35-50 minutes or until golden brown and firm.

INGREDIENTS

4 green onions; whites and light green parts finely sliced

1 clove garlic; minced

2 Tablespoons butter

2 Tablespoons white wine

2 Tablespoons fresh dill

3/4 cup cooked baby shrimp

3/4 cup cooked lump crab meat

3 large eggs

1 cup heavy cream

1/2 cup whole milk

1/2 teaspoon salt

Ground white pepper to taste

1/2 cup Swiss or Gruyére cheese

1 Pillsbury Ready Pie Crust

E ELECTRIC EATS   Supper Time! Entrées for All!

91

Broiled Salmon with Gingered Balsamic Vinegar Sauce

INGREDIENTS

4 salmon fillets, about 6 ounces each; skin in tact

1/4 teaspoon salt

Freshly ground black pepper

Gingered Balsamic Vinegar Sauce (recipe below)

Gingered Balsamic Vinegar Sauce:

1/4 cup balsamic vinegar

1 tablespoon fresh ginger; grated

1 tablespoon minced green onion

1 clove garlic; minced

It's the sauce that makes this dish so special and gourmet-tasting! Do not omit it or you'll be sorry!

PREPARATION:

Wash, pat dry and season the fillets with salt and pepper.

Preheat your broiler.

Spray the broiler insert or a shallow baking dish with non-stick cooking spray.

Arrange salmon fillets, skin-side down, on the pan. Place into your oven about 6 inches from the broiler, close the door, leaving a crack, and broil, just until opaque, 5-7 minutes, or until the fish will flake using the tip of a knife.

Place on warm platter and pour sauce overall.

GINGERED BALSAMIC VINEGAR SAUCE:

Bring all ingredients to a simmer in a small non-reactive skillet. Simmer 5 minutes, remove from heat and pour over grilled fish.

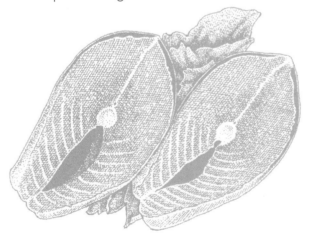

92

Supper Time! Entrées for All!   ELECTRIC EATS E

Fried Oyster Po' Boys

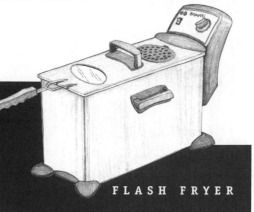

INGREDIENTS

1 pint shucked oysters; drained, washed and drained again

3/4 cup flour

3/4 cup yellow cornmeal

1 teaspoon salt

1/2 teaspoon cayenne pepper

1/4 teaspoon fresh ground black pepper

Oil for frying

2 soft hoagie rolls

1 tomato; sliced

1 cup shredded iceberg lettuce

Tartar sauce or seafood sauce

Tarter Sauce:

1 Cup Mayonnaise

1 1/4 teaspoon lemon juice

4-5 large sweet gherkin pickles

2 Tablespoons Capers

2 Tablespoon Dijon mustard

1/4 small onion

Seafood Sauce:

1 cup mayonnaise

1/4 cup ketchup

1/4 cup chili sauce

2 tablespoon vegetable oil

1 clove garlic

1/2 small onion

1 tablespoon vinegar

1/2 cup parsley

1/2 teaspoon dry mustard

1/4 teaspoon paprika

1 tsp. Worcestershire sauce

Juice of 1/2 lemon

Dash Tabasco sauce

Make this when you want to take an imaginary trip to New Orleans!

PREPARATION:

Preheat your Flash Fryer to 375°.

Make the Tartar Sauce or Seafood Sauce (see next page).

Combine the flour, corn meal, salt, pepper and cayenne pepper in a large zip-top bag.

Gently pat dry the washed oysters and put them in with the breading mixture. Toss to coat.

Lower the fry basket into the hot oil. Using tongs gently remove the oysters from the breading and shake off the excess. Drop the breaded oysters, one at a time, into the hot oil; you may have to fry in batches so as not to over-crowd the fryer. Shake the basket to prevent them from sticking together or to the bottom of the basket.

Fry for 2-3 minutes or until lightly browned. Drain on paper towels.

Split the hoagie rolls lengthwise and spread 1-2 Tablespoons tartar sauce or seafood sauce on each side. Place the oysters in the center and top with shredded lettuce and tomato slices.

TARTER SAUCE:

You can easily make this with your food processor! Use with fish, fried seafood or with crab cakes.

Place all ingredients into a food processor. Process on the lowest speed using the pulse button until the pickles and onions are into small bits the mixture is smooth. Chill before using.

TARTER SAUCE:

This is a great sauce to serve with crab cakes, fish or any time you want an alternative to tartar sauce.

Place all ingredients together in a blender or food processor. Blend until creamy. Refrigerate until ready to serve.

Shrimp & Artichoke Stuffed Red Peppers

INGREDIENTS

2 cups cooked small shrimp; shelled and deveined

2 cups cooked white rice

1 cup sliced black olives

2 8-ounce cans tomato sauce; reserve 1/2 cup

1 14-ounce can artichokes; drained and chopped

1 teaspoon salt

1/4 teaspoon red pepper flakes

1/2 teaspoon onion salt

1/2 teaspoon coarse ground black pepper

1/2 - 3/4 cup shredded cheddar cheese

6 large red bell peppers

Looking for something different to serve? Try this and I'll bet you'll add it to your monthly meals!

PREPARATION:

Preheat convection oven to 350°. Grease the bottom of a 9x9-inch baking dish with shortening.

Remove the tops of the peppers and scrape out the seeds and membranes; set aside.

Combine the shrimp, rice, olives, all but 1/2 cup of the tomato sauce, artichokes, salt, red pepper flakes, onion salt and pepper in a mixing bowl. Mix well.

Stuff each pepper with the mixture and place into the baking dish. Spoon a little of the remaining tomato sauce on top of each stuffed pepper.

Cover with aluminum foil and bake 30 minutes.

Uncover, sprinkle the cheese on top of each pepper and bake another 15 minutes or until the cheese is melted and beginning to brown.

Broiled White Fish

For a quick, low-carbohydrate meal try this no-fail recipe!

PREPARATION:

Preheat your broiler to 450°.

Line the shallow broiler pan that came with your oven with aluminum foil. You make use a different foil-lined dish if you prefer.

Wash and pat dry the fish fillets. Lightly salt and pepper both sides and place into pan.

Melt the butter in a measuring cup in your microwave. Add in the wine, Worcestershire sauce, garlic salt, lemon juice and chopped parsley. Blend together with a fork and pour over the fish. Top each filet with a sprinkling of paprika.

Broil about 6 inches from the heat source for 10 – 12 minutes, without turning, or until fish is done and will flake easily.

Serve with fresh lemon wedges.

INGREDIENTS

4 medium white fish fillets (trout, tilapia, cod, sea bass, etc.)

Salt and pepper

1/2 stick butter or margarine

1 Tablespoon white wine (optional)

2 teaspoon Worcestershire sauce

1 teaspoon garlic salt

1 Tablespoon lemon juice

1 Tablespoon chopped parsley

Paprika

1 lemon cut into wedges; seeds removed

Garlic Shrimp

INGREDIENTS

1 pound medium shrimp; shelled and deveined

1 stick butter

4 cloves garlic; minced

1/4 cup red bell pepper; chopped

1/4 cup white wine

2 teaspoons lemon juice

1 Tablespoons parsley flakes

1/2 teaspoon crushed red pepper flakes

1/2 teaspoon salt

8-ounces angle hair pasta

This is a fast way to make a great topping for pasta!

PREPARATION:

Preheat broiler to 450°.

Cook pasta according to package directions. Drain and place into a pasta bowl. Cover with a kitchen towel to keep warm.

Wash and pat dry the shrimp. Place, in a single layer, in a shallow baking pan; set aside.

Melt the butter over medium heat in a medium skillet. Add the garlic and the red pepper and cook 2-3 minutes until pepper is cooked but still crisp and garlic is not browned yet.

Add the white wine and simmer 2-3 minutes more. Stir in the lemon juice, parsley flakes, red pepper flakes and salt.

Pour mixture over shrimp and place about 4-inches under the broiler. Cook for 3 minutes, turn and cook another minute or two. Shrimp should be pink and starting to brown.

Remove from oven and toss with the angel hair pasta. Serve immediately with parmesan cheese.

English Battered Fish

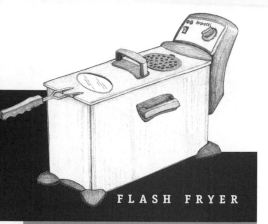

INGREDIENTS

3 pounds white fish fillets
1 cup all-purpose flour
Oil for frying

English Fish Batter:
2/3 cup flat beer
1/3 cup lemon juice
1 egg
1/2 cup self-rising flour
Salt and pepper to taste

I had many requests to keep this recipe in all my books, so here it is!

PREPARATION:

Wash your fish fillets and while they are still moist, lightly flour and set them on a wire rack to dry.

When they are dry, dip one piece at a time into the batter described below and fry in a pan for 4 minutes per side or in your deep fryer at 375°f for 7-8 minutes.

Remove from oil and drain on a paper towel.

ENGLISH FISH BATTER:

If you want fish like they have in England, you must use this batter! But, the English aren't the only ones known for their fried fish! In Florida, we have a local fish, the light delicious Black Grouper, which makes a great sandwich when fried using this batter.

Mix the beer (any brand), lemon juice and self-rising flour in a large mixing bowl with a wire whisk. Whip the mixture until completely mixed. Let stand at room temperature for 10 minutes before using.

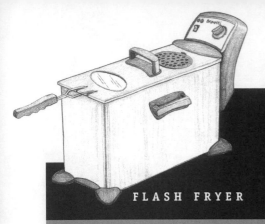

Southern-Fried Fish

INGREDIENTS

6 1/2-inch thick fish fillets; whatever is fresh in your area

1 cup milk

1 1/2 cups yellow corn meal

1/2 cup flour

1 1/2 teaspoons salt

1/2 teaspoon paprika

1 teaspoon lemon pepper

Vegetable oil for frying

This is the staple recipe I use in my Flash Fryer on HSN and it always comes out great! It also reminds me of summers with my family fishing adventures!

PREPARATION:

Wash and pat dry the fish. Place the fish in a zip-type plastic bag and pour in milk. Seal the bag and refrigerate 30 minutes.

Preheat your Flash Fryer to 360°.

In a large plastic bag, mix together the cornmeal, flour, salt, paprika and lemon pepper.

Remove 3 fillets from the milk and pat dry. Place in the bag with the cornmeal mixture and shake well to thoroughly coat. Let the fish sit in the bag for 4 or 5 minutes.

Lower the basket into your flash fryer.

Give the fillets a final shake in the bag and remove with long tongs; shake off excess breading. Gently place, one at a time, into the hot oil.

Fry for 6 -8 minutes or until the fish is a light golden brown.

Serve with tartar sauce (see index) or lemon wedges.

98

Supper Time! Entrées for All! ELECTRIC EATS E

Baked Cherrystone Clams with Spicy Butter

CONVECTION OVEN

I wasn't sure whether to put these under the appetizer section or the meals. I like them so much that I make a meal out of them so here they are!

PREPARATION:

Preheat broiler to 450°.

Rinse and drain the clams to remove any sand. Open them and discard the top shell. Place them on the half shell neatly on a baking sheet.

Place the remaining ingredients into your food processor. Process for 45 seconds to a minute until everything is well blended.

Spoon the mixture evenly over the clams. Squeeze a little lemon juice on each clam.

Place them under the broiler for about 2 minutes.

Serve immediately with hot crusty bread.

INGREDIENTS

36 cherrystone clams

1 small onion; finely chopped

2 cloves garlic; finely chopped (1 Tablespoon)

2 sticks butter; room temperature

4 drops Tabasco Sauce

1 Tablespoon Worcestershire Sauce

1 Tablespoon Dijon mustard

2 Tablespoons fresh parsley; chopped

2 Tablespoons fresh basil; chopped

2 Tablespoons parmesan cheese

Salt and fresh ground black pepper to taste

1 lemon, cut to squeeze

E **ELECTRIC EATS** Supper Time! Entrées for All!

99

ON THE SIDE!
VEGGIES GALORE

Creamed Spinach

INGREDIENTS

10 oz. frozen spinach; thawed and patted dry

3 Tbs. soft butter

1 clove garlic; very finely minced

1/2 small white onion; very finely minced

2 Tbs. flour

3/4 cup milk

4 ounces cream cheese

1/2 tsp. salt

1/4 tsp. paprika

1/4 tsp. dry mustard

1/4 cup grated Parmesan cheese

1/4 cup seasoned breadcrumbs

4 Tbs. butter; cut into small pieces

I love creamed spinach. To me, it is the ultimate comfort food–plus, it's good for me! it's good for you, too!

PREPARATION:

Preheat convection oven to 350°.

Process spinach, in your food processor, until almost pureed. Place in fine colander and squeeze out any remaining liquid; set aside.

Use your food processor and finely mince the garlic and onion.

In a skillet, over medium heat, melt the butter along with the minced garlic and onion; stir constantly until butter is completely melted and bubbly. Stir in flour until blended. Slowly add the milk stirring constantly. Add the cream cheese, salt and paprika and allow mixture to heat until cheese is just melted. When the sauce is hot and smooth, stir in spinach and cook 3 minutes.

Transfer to a greased 8î baking dish and evenly sprinkle top with Parmesan cheese, breadcrumbs and butter pieces.

Bake for 15 minutes or until bubbly.

102

On the Side! Veggies Galore! ELECTRIC EATS E

Cauliflower or Broccoli Au Gratin

This dish is so good, even the kids will eat their veggies!

PREPARATION:

Preheat convection oven to 350°.

Bring the cauliflower, 1 1/2 cups water and 1/2 tsp. salt to a full boil. Cook for 5 minutes if using cauliflower and 3 minutes if using broccoli. Pour into a colander and drain.

In a small saucepan, blend butter, flour, salt, pepper, onion powder and dry mustard together over medium heat. Add cold milk and cook slowly, stirring frequently until a smooth sauce is achieved. Add the cheese and parsley; cook until cheese is melted.

Pour a small amount of sauce into a lightly greased casserole dish; then add a layer of cauliflower or broccoli. Continue, alternating layers of sauce and vegetable, making the last layer sauce.

Crumble a small amount of cornflakes and sprinkle over the top. Shake paprika over all and bake 20 to 30 minutes.

INGREDIENTS

1 large head cauliflower or broccoli; cut into flowerets

1 1/2 cups water

1/2 tsp. salt

6 Tbsp. butter

4 Tbsp. flour

1/2 tsp. salt

1/4 tsp pepper

1/4 tsp. onion powder

1/4 tsp. dry mustard

2 cups cold milk

1 cup sharp cheddar cheese

4 Tbsp. minced parsley

Cornflakes; crumbled

Paprika

E ELECTRIC EATS   On the Side! Veggies Galore!

103

Macaroni & Cheese

INGREDIENTS

8 oz. elbow macaroni

2 Tablespoons butter

1 Tablespoon flour

1 1/3 cups milk

2 Tbsp. grated onion

1/2 teaspoon salt

1/8 tsp. cayenne pepper

1/4 tsp. dry mustard

1 cup sharp cheddar cheese; shredded

1 cup Monterey Jack cheese; shredded

1 8-ounce block Velveeta cheese

1/2 cup dry breadcrumbs

2 Tbs. butter

Paprika

I've updated my macaroni and cheese recipe! I didn't think I could ever improve on this recipe, but I think I have!

PREPARATION:

Preheat convection oven to 350°.

Lightly butter an 8x8-inch baking dish.

Boil macaroni according to the package directions. Blanch in cold water to prevent sticking; set aside.

In a medium sauce pan, over medium heat, melt 2 tablespoons butter. Add the flour and make a paste. Slowly pour in the milk, stirring constantly. Add the onion, salt, cayenne and mustard. Reduce heat to medium low and add cheeses. Cook mixture until cheeses are melted.

Remove pan from heat. Add the cooked macaroni and toss to coat. Pour mixture into the prepared pan.

Sprinkle breadcrumbs evenly on top and dot with the butter; lightly sprinkle paprika over all.

Bake 30-40 minutes or until bubbly and lightly browned on top.

104

On the Side! Veggies Galore! ELECTRIC EATS E

Sweet Potato & Pecan Casserole

You have to have this on your Thanksgiving table! Marshmallows are optional!

PREPARATION:

Preheat convection oven to 325°.

Place 2 cups of the pecan halves into your food processor. Pulse twice; does not over-chop!

Drain the canned sweet potatoes and add to the processor with the pecans. Add the remaining ingredients (except marshmallows) and process just until smooth.

Pour the potato mixture into a lightly greased 9x13-inch baking dish

Place the remaining pecan halves on top in a decorative manner.

Bake 30 minutes.

When the edges appear cooked, top with marshmallows and continue cooking until marshmallows are golden brown.

INGREDIENTS

3 cups pecan halves

1 40-oz. can sweet potatoes (or 3 large sweet potatoes, peeled, boiled and drained)

2 cups milk

4 eggs; well beaten

8 tablespoons butter or margarine; melted

1 cup granulated sugar

1/2 cup light brown sugar; packed

1/4 teaspoon ground cloves

1/2 teaspoon ground nutmeg

1 teaspoon ground cinnamon

Miniature marshmallows (optional)

Perfect Mashed Potatoes

INGREDIENTS

2 pounds potatoes; peeled and diced

4 Tablespoons butter

About 3/4 cup warm milk

1/2 teaspoon salt

1/4 teaspoon fresh ground black pepper

2 whole raw eggs (optional)

A few sprigs fresh parsley; chopped

Perfect mashed potatoes are wonderful! The trick is to use the right potato with the right starch content. I find that the red-skinned potato or the Yukon gold works best! I also add egg to my mashed potatoes, but you can omit them if you prefer.

PREPARATION:

Place the potatoes and the whole eggs (optional) into a large pot and cover with cold water. Place the pot over high heat and bring to a boil. Reduce heat to medium-high and continue to gently boil until potatoes are fork tender. Do not overcook!

Remove 4 Tablespoons of the water from the pot and set aside. Drain the potatoes through a colander.

Remove the eggs and run under cold water. Peel the eggs and chop fine.

Place the potatoes back into the pot or into a mixing bowl. Add the reserved liquid, the butter, 1/2 cup of the milk, salt, pepper and the chopped egg.

Use your hand mixer on the lowest speed and begin to mix the potatoes. Continue to add the milk until a smooth creamy texture is achieved; you may not use all of the milk.

Taste the mixture and add additional salt and/or pepper if desired. Use a spoon and stir in the chopped parsley.

106

On the Side! Veggies Galore!   ELECTRIC EATS   E

Potato Pancakes

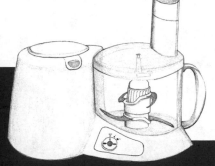

If you are tired of potatoes baked, mashed and fried, try these instead! They make a great side dish with everything from burgers to ham!

PREPARATION:

Wash, peel and place the potatoes into ice water for 15 minutes. Remove from water and pat dry.

Use the large shredding attachment on your food processor, or hand shredder, and shred the potatoes. Immediately place them back into a bowl of ice water and let them sit 45 minutes.

Drain the potatoes well and pat dry with a paper towel.

Beat the eggs, flour, onion, salt and pepper together in a medium mixing bowl. Add the potatoes and mix well.

Heat a thin layer of oil in a heavy, non-stick fry pan over medium heat. Using a tablespoon from your utensils, drop a heaping spoonful into the oil; flatten slightly with the back of the spoon. You can make 3-4 at a time depending on your pan size, but do not crowd the pan.

Cook until golden brown (about 3-4 minutes) and then flip over and cook the other side.

Drain on a paper towel and keep warm in the oven until all the pancakes are made. When you are ready to serve them, sprinkle one side lightly with paprika.

INGREDIENTS

2 pounds red-skinned or Yukon Gold potatoes

1/2 cup self rising flour

2 eggs

1 Tablespoon onion; finely minced

1/2 teaspoon salt

Fresh ground pepper to taste

Oil for shallow pan frying

Paprika

Easy Corn Bake

INGREDIENTS

1/2 cup melted butter

2 eggs

2 Tablespoons chopped pimento (optional)

1 package (8.5 ounce) corn bread mix

1 15-ounce can whole kernel corn, drained

1 14.75-ounce can creamed corn

3/4 cup sour cream

1/4 cup milk

1/2 teaspoon salt

1 teaspoon sugar

I can't remember the first time I made this dish, but I know how much I like it...lots!!!! It's easy and something different than plain 'ole canned corn.

PREPARATION:

Preheat convection oven to 350°.

Lightly grease a 9x9-inch baking dish.

Use the lowest speed of your hand mixer, or a wooden spoon, and combine all of the ingredients together in a medium mixing bowl.

Spread the mixture into the prepared pan.

Bake 35 minutes or until top is golden brown.

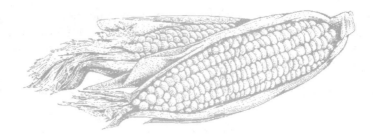

108

Cheesy Broccoli & Rice Casserole

This is a great dish to take along to a get-together because no one ever brings it but everyone likes it! It is also good at home served with chicken!

PREPARATION:

Preheat convection oven to 350°.

Lightly grease 9x13-inch baking dish.

Cook broccoli and rice according to package directions. Drain broccoli, if necessary.

Place carrots into a microwave safe container with 2 Tablespoons water, cover and cook 3 minutes on highest setting; drain.

In a medium saucepan, over low heat the soups with the water until hot but not boiling. Add the cheese and stir until melted. Remove from heat.

Melt butter with the oil in a skillet over medium-high heat and sauté the onion with the carrots until onions are tender.

In a large mixing bowl combine the broccoli, rice, vegetables and cheese mixture. Pour mixture into prepared pan.

Bake 15 minutes until bubbly and lightly browned.

INGREDIENTS

2 10-ounce packages frozen chopped broccoli

3 cups instant rice

1 10.75-ounce can condensed cream of mushroom soup

1 10.75-ounce can condensed cream of chicken soup

2 1/2 cups water

1 8-ounce block Velveeta cheese, cubed

1 Tablespoon butter

1 Tablespoon olive oil

1 cup chopped carrots

1/2 cup finely chopped onion

1/2 teaspoon salt

1/4 teaspoon ground black pepper

Beefy Baked Beans

INGREDIENTS

1 pound ground beef

1 53-oz. can Pork 'n Beans

1 16-ounce can pinto beans; drained

1 medium onion

2 teaspoons dried mustard

1/4 cup packed brown sugar

3 tablespoons ketchup

2 tablespoons Worcestershire sauce

1/2 teaspoon salt

1/2 teaspoon liquid smoke

Pinch cinnamon

I have always received complements on my baked beans. I hope you like them as well! The ground beef makes it hearty enough to almost stand alone.

PREPARATION:

Preheat convection oven to 350°.

Cook the ground beef until done in a large skillet. Drain and crumble the beef.

Cut both ends off the onion and peel. Starting at the large end, cut 4 thin slices; set aside. Finely chop the remaining of the onion.

In a large mixing bowl, stir together the pork 'n beans and their juices and the drained pinto beans. Stir in crumbled beef, chopped onion, mustard, brown sugar, ketchup, Worcestershire sauce, salt, liquid smoke and a pinch of cinnamon

Pour the mixture into a 9x9-inch baking dish. Separate the onion rings and scatter over the beans.

Bake for 35-45 minutes or until onion is brown and the beans are bubbly hot.

110

On the Side! Veggies Galore! ELECTRIC EATS E

Cole Slaw

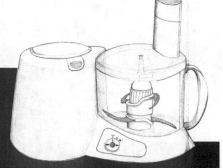

A must have at any cookout or picnic, but equally good served as a side dish for dinner. To me, the key to good Cole Slaw is to slice the cabbage very, very thin and to pick out any large or tough pieces of cabbage; that way the salad will be light with no overpowering cabbage taste!

PREPARATION:

Use your food processor to shred the carrots and cabbage or prepare by hand.

Toss the prepared cabbage and carrots together in a large bowl. In a small bowl, mix together the remaining ingredients until well blended. Add to the cabbage and carrots and toss until cabbage is completely coated.

Refrigerate 2-3 hours or overnight and toss again before serving.

MAYONNAISE:

Basic mayonnaise is the base to many salad dressings. Try adding herbs, garlic, extra lemon or horseradish to spice it up!

Place the egg, lemon or vinegar, salt and 2 tablespoons of the oil into a blender or food processor fitted with a dough or whipping blade. Whip at high speed until slightly thickened. With machine still running at high speed, slowly drizzle in the remaining oil until the mayonnaise is thick. Refrigerate.

INGREDIENTS

1 medium head cabbage; cored and thinly shredded (about 6 cups packed)

1 cup carrots; finely chopped or shredded, rinsed and patted dry

1 cup mayonnaise (homemade or store-bought)

2 tablespoon milk

2 tablespoons sweet pickle juice

1/4 teaspoon salt

1 lg. dash white pepper

1/2 teaspoon lemon juice

1 teaspoon sugar

Mayonnaise:

1 egg

1/2 teaspoon lemon juice or white vinegar

1 cup good oil; vegetable or olive

1/2 teaspoon salt

Red Potato Salad with Dill

INGREDIENTS

10-12 small red new potatoes

1/2 cup mayonnaise (homemade or store bought)

1 cup sour cream

1/2 teaspoon salt

1 tablespoon fresh dill weed, or more to taste

1/4 teaspoon black pepper

1/4 teaspoon prepared horseradish

This salad is great cold, but is also delicious hot when served with a beef roast! The dill gives it a wonderful flavor and makes it a pretty salad to serve.

PREPARATION:

Wash and quarter the potatoes. Cook in lightly salted boiling water until just tender. Plunge potatoes into ice water. Drain and put into a medium serving bowl.

In a small mixing bowl, mix the remaining ingredients together thoroughly. Gently stir the mixture into the potatoes; cover and refrigerate until cold. Serve.

TO SERVE HOT:

Do not plunge the potatoes into ice water; put them directly into a serving bowl. Dollop the creamy topping on top of the hot potatoes, or pass around separately and let everyone top their own potatoes!

Hot German-Style Potato Salad

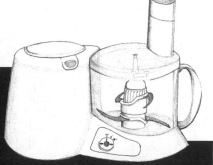

I love to serve this salad with a thick Rueben sandwich on a cold day! If my Brother John is around, I always have to make double because he likes it so much!

PREPARATION:

Gently boil potatoes, with skins on, until tender. Peel and slice thin while still hot; set aside.

In medium skillet, cook bacon until crispy. Remove bacon from skillet, reserving drippings, and chop.

Add the chopped onion to the drippings in the pan and sauté until golden. Add the chopped bacon, the chopped pickle and the remaining ingredients and cook until hot and bubbly.

Toss in the potatoes until heated throughout. Serve hot.

INGREDIENTS

6 medium sized all-purpose potatoes
4 strips bacon
1/4 cup onion; chopped
1 dill pickle; chopped
1/4 cup water
1/2 cup vinegar
1/2 teaspoon sugar
1/2 teaspoon salt
1/4 teaspoon celery seed
1/4 teaspoon dry mustard

FANTASTIC FINISHES!
DESSERTS & SWEETS

Bravetti Big Batch of Cookies

INGREDIENTS

1 cup light brown sugar (firmly packed)

1 cup granulated sugar

4 sticks of butter or margarine

4 large eggs

1 1/2 tsp. vanilla

4 1/2 cups all-purpose flour

1 tablespoon baking soda

1 tablespoon baking powder

1 cup chocolate chips

1 cup peanut butter candies or M&M's

1 cup coarsely chopped walnuts

These are the cookies I always make on HSN to demonstrate the power of the Bravetti Hand Mixers! They taste so good, people place dibs on the dough to take home and bake with their families! I usually give it to my good friend Carol Graff; she is a very talented Food Stylist at HSN and gives me invaluable help!

PREPARATION:

Preheat your convection oven to 350° or your conventional oven to 375°.

In a large bowl, beat the sugars, butter, eggs and vanilla until creamy using your hand mixer. Switch mixer to low speed and add the flour, baking soda and baking powder and mix until cookie dough is smooth.

Remove the beaters from your mixer and insert the dough hooks. Add the candy, chips and nuts; blend just until mixed.

Drop rounded teaspoons of dough onto an un-greased cookie sheet. Bake for 8-10 minutes or until light golden brown.

Let cool on cookie sheet for 5 minutes and then transfer to a cooling rack. Store cookies in an airtight container.

Food Processor Cookies

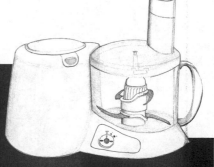

This recipe does not make as much as the Bravetti Big Batch of Cookies, but it is so easy and fast, you can easily make 2 batches.

PREPARATION:

Preheat your convection oven to 350° or your conventional oven to 375°.

In a large measuring cup or bowl, stir together the flour, baking soda, baking powder and salt; set aside.

Place your dough blade into your food processor. Add evenly to the bottom, in the order listed, white sugar, brown sugar, butter, eggs and vanilla. Pulse a few times and then turn processor to low speed until well blended.

With processor running at low speed, begin to pour the flour down the feed tube. As the mixture gets thick, adjust the speed faster. Continue to do this until the mixture is smooth.

Stop the processor and remove lid. Pour the chocolate chips, candies and nuts evenly over the top of the batter. Replace lid and pulse until blended. Stop processor, remove lid and blade. Use a spoon to finish mixing in the candies, if needed.

Drop rounded teaspoons of dough onto an un-greased cookie sheet. Bake for 8-10 minutes or until light golden brown. Let cool on cookie sheet for 5 minutes and then transfer to a cooling rack. Store cookies in an airtight container.

INGREDIENTS

3/4 cup white sugar

3/4 cup brown sugar

2 sticks butter; slightly softened and cut in half

2 eggs

2 teaspoons vanilla extract

2 cups flour

2 teaspoons baking powder

2 teaspoons baking soda

1/4 teaspoon salt

3/4 cup chocolate. Chips

3/4 cup M&M's

1/2 cup chopped walnuts

Cranberry Chip Cookies

INGREDIENTS

- 3/4 cup light brown sugar, firmly packed
- 3/4 cup granulated sugar
- 3/4 cup butter flavored Crisco
- 2 teaspoons vanilla
- 2 eggs
- 2 cups flour
- 1/2 teaspoon salt
- 1/2 teaspoon baking powder
- 1/2 teaspoon baking soda
- 1 cup white chocolate chips
- 1 cup dries cranberries
- 1/2 cup chopped walnuts (optional)

I like these better than chocolate chip cookies!

PREPARATION:

Preheat oven to 375°.

Using your hand mixer, blend the sugars with the Crisco until light and fluffy. Add in the vanilla and eggs and beat until creamy.

Sift together the flour, baking powder, baking soda and salt and the blend into the sugar mixture.

Switch to your dough hooks and blend in the cranberries, chocolate chips and, if desired, the walnuts.

Drop rounded teaspoons of dough onto an un-greased cookie sheet. Bake for 8-10 minutes or until light golden brown.

Let cool on cookie sheet for 5 minutes and then transfer to a cooling rack. Store cookies in an airtight container.

No-Bake Chocolate Oatmeal Cookies

I first made this recipe on HSN to demonstrate the power of my mixer, then I tasted it; it was love at first bite! I roll the cookies in shredded coconut for added color on camera, and because I like coconut, but you can omit this step if desired!

PREPARATION:

Place the sugar, cocoa, butter and milk into a medium saucepan and slowly bring to a gentle boil; stirring frequently. Remove from heat and allow to cool 5-10 minutes.

In a large mixing bowl, use your hand mixer to combine the oatmeal, peanut butter and vanilla. Pour the warm chocolate mixture into the oatmeal mixture and continue to mix, on low, until everything is thoroughly combined.

While the mixture is still warm, form small balls and then roll them into the shredded coconut. Place on waxed paper and allow to cool completely.

INGREDIENTS

2 cups granulated sugar

3 tablespoons cocoa

1/4 cup butter

1/2 cup milk

3 cups oatmeal, quick cook style

1 teaspoon vanilla

1/2 cup peanut butter, homemade is best

1 cup shredded coconut

Blueberry & Peach Cobbler

INGREDIENTS

2 cups fresh or frozen cling peach sliced; thawed

1 cup fresh or frozen blueberries; thawed

1 cup sugar

1 cup flour

1 cup milk

1 teaspoon vanilla extract

1/4 teaspoon salt

1 1/2 tablespoon baking powder

1 cup sugar

1 stick butter

To me, nothing is better than a good cobbler! This is my absolute favorite one with the combination of peaches and blueberries!

PREPARATION:

Preheat your convection oven to 325° or your conventional oven to 350°.

Mix fruit with 1 cup sugar; set aside.

In a medium mixing bowl, use your hand mixer on low speed, to blend flour, milk, vanilla extract, salt, baking powder and remaining 1 cup sugar, until thick; set batter aside.

Place the stick of butter into the bottom of a 9" x 9" x 4" pan and put into preheated oven.

When butter has melted, remove pan from oven and pour batter into pan with the butter; do not mix. Pour fruit and sugar mixture over all. Return to oven and bake for 1 hour.

This cobbler is delicious hot or cold, served alone or topped with cream, milk or ice cream.

Honey Shortcakes with Fresh Fruit

These shortcakes are light and spongy with a touch-of-honey taste that is perfect on hot days. Serve with cold fresh fruit like strawberries, kiwi, banana, pineapple or a combination!

PREPARATION:

Grease and flour a 6-cup jumbo muffin tin or 6 10-ounce custard cups.

Preheat your convection oven to 325° or your conventional oven to 350°.

Beat eggs in a medium bowl, or the bowl of your hand-stand mixer, on medium speed until the eggs are thick; about 3-4 minutes. Gradually add the sugar, while continuing to mix, until the mixture is light and fluffy.

Turn the mixer to low speed and add the honey. When the honey is mixed in, add in the flour, baking powder and salt and continue to mix until just blended.

In a small sauce pan, heat and stir milk and butter, over low heat, until butter has just melted. Add to the mixture, beating until well combined. Pour batter into prepared cups. Bake 15 to 20 minutes or until top springs back when touched. Cool cakes in pans on wire rack for 10 minutes, remove from pan and place cakes on wire rack until completely cool.

Place cakes on a platter or individual plates. Toss the fresh fruit with the 2 Tbs. honey, lemon peel and lemon juice. Spoon fruit over cakes and top with whipped cream if desired.

2 eggs; at room temperature

1 cup flour

1 teaspoon baking powder

1/4 teaspoon salt

3/4 cup sugar

1/4 cup honey

1/2 cup milk

2 Tablespoons butter

2 Tablespoons honey

1 teaspoon lemon peel; finely shredded

1 Tablespoon lemon juice

3 cups fresh fruit

Sweetened whipped cream or non-dairy whipped topping (optional)

Sticky Toffee Pudding

INGREDIENTS

1 cup toasted walnuts; chopped

1 1/2 sticks (3/4 cup) butter

1 cup light brown sugar

4 Tablespoons cream

2 Tablespoons lemon juice

2 eggs

1 cup self rising flour

This dessert is soooo incredibly good! I make it using my Bravetti Steamer because it easier and takes much less time. If you do not have a steamer, follow the alternate directions below.

PREPARATION:

Fill your steamer with water and place on one basket and the lid; do not turn on yet.

Grease a 2-pint glass Pyrex (oven-safe) deep bowl with shortening. Add half of the nuts to the bottom of the bowl; set aside.

Heat in a small saucepan 4 Tablespoons of the butter with 4 Tablespoons of the brown sugar, the cream and 1 Tablespoon lemon juice. Cook the mixture over low heat, stirring often, until it is smooth. Pour half of the mixture into the greased bowl and swirl around to coat the sides. Set the remaining sauce aside.

Use your hand mixer and beat until light, the remaining butter and brown sugar. Gradually beat in the eggs. When smooth, turn mixer to low and add the flour, remaining nuts and lemon juice; beat until well blended. Pour the batter into the bowl atop the hot mixture.

Cover the bowl with waxed paper and secure with string or a rubber band. Place the bowl into the steamer basket, put on lid and turn steamer on. Steam 45-50 minutes until the center is set.

Just before serving, reheat the remaining sauce. Unmold the pudding onto a warm plate and pour warmed sauce over all.

NO STEAMER DIRECTIONS:

Place the covered dish into a pan with 2-3 inches of water. Steam in the oven at 350° for 1 1/4 - 1 1/2 hours until the center is set. Unmold and serve as directed above.

Apple Brown Betty – English Style

This dessert is sure to please anyone that likes apples! I serve it topped with vanilla ice cream.

PREPARATION:

Preheat convection oven to 350° or conventional oven to 375°.

Butter a 9 x 9-inch, oven safe deep dish.

Combine the sugar, cinnamon, nutmeg and cloves in a small bowl and set aside.

Cut the butter into tiny pieces and set aside.

Peel, core and slice the apples. Immediately toss with the lemon juice and sprinkle with the granulated sugar.

Sprinkle 3 Tablespoons of the breadcrumbs into the prepared dish. Cover with 1/3 pf the apples and sprinkle with 1/3 of the sugar and spice mixture. Add another layer breadcrumbs and dot with 1/3 of the butter.

Repeat the layers 2 more times ending with a layer of breadcrumbs. Sprinkle the nuts on top and dot with the remaining butter.

Bake 30-35 minutes, until the apples are tender and the top is golden brown. Serve warm with vanilla ice cream.

INGREDIENTS

1 cup plain bread crumbs

3/4 cup brown sugar

1/2 teaspoon cinnamon

1/4 teaspoon nutmeg

1/4 teaspoon ground cloves

6 Tablespoons butter; cold

2 pounds granny smith apples

2 Tablespoons lemon juice

1 Tablespoon granulated sugar

1/2 cup walnuts; finely chopped

Vanilla ice cream

Frozen Fluffer-Nutter Pie

INGREDIENTS

15.0-ounce box Jell-O Instant Chocolate Pudding mix

2 1/2 cups cold milk

1 cup marshmallow cream

1/2 cup creamy peanut butter

Chopped peanuts (optional)

Graham Cracker Crust:

1 cup graham cracker crumbs

1/2 stick (4 Tablespoons) margarine

2 Tablespoons granulated sugar

I was looking for a new demonstration for a hand-stand mixer and decided to combine my son Max's favorite things—chocolate, peanut butter and marshmallow cream. This is the result and I (and Max) think it is great!

PREPARATION:

Place the gram cracker crumbs into the bottom of a 9-inch pie pan. Melt the margarine and add it to the crumbs. Add the sugar. Mix with a fork until well blended. Press the crumbs evenly across the bottoms and side of the pie pan. Set aside.

Pour the milk into the metal bowl of your hand-stand mixer, or in a medium mixing bowl. Add half the pudding mix at a time and blend, using the lowest speed of your mixer, until all the powder is incorporated.

Turn the mixer to the highest speed and blend for 2-3 minutes or until pudding begins to thicken.

Turn the mixer to a medium speed and add in the marshmallow cream and peanut butter. Blend until well mixed.

Pour the mixture into the prepared pie pan and place in the freezer. Freeze for at least 1 hour.

To serve, remove from freezer and let sit 10- 15 minutes before cutting into wedges.

Mandarin Orange Parfait

This dessert is cool and light for a summer time cookout! It is especially easy if you buy the snack-size prepared Jell-O cups from the store!

2 cups heavy whipping cream

1/4 cup Confectioner's sugar

4 orange-flavored Jell-O gelatin cups

1 11-ounce can mandarin orange segments; drained

PREPARATION:

Pour the whipping cream into the metal bowl of your hand-stand mixer, or use a medium mixing bowl. Beat the cream on highest speed for 1 1/2 - 2 minutes or until cream is very thick.

Add the powdered sugar and Jell-O and blend on low until mixed in; scrape the sides and bottom if necessary.

Add the mandarin oranges and blend just until incorporated.

Spoon the parfait into single serving dishes or glasses. Serve immediately or cover and refrigerate until ready to serve.

STRAWBERRY PARFAIT:

Try this variation of the Mandarin Orange Parfait if you prefer strawberries over oranges! Just follow the directions above but use:

4 strawberry-flavored Jell-O gelatin cups (instead of orange)
1 cup fresh strawberries; sliced or chopped (instead of the mandarin oranges)

Easy Lemon Meringue Pie

INGREDIENTS

Filling:

1 can sweetened condensed milk

1/2 cup lemon juice

1 teaspoon lemon zest

3 egg yolks

1 8-inch pre-baked pie crust (cooled) or crumb crust

1 meringue recipe (follows)

Meringue:

6 egg whites

1/4 cup sugar

Pinch of cream of tartar (if you live in a high-humidity area)

Who doesn't love this traditional pie? It's equally great for nice dinner parties, outdoor picnics or anything in between! Plus, this recipe is so easy; you won't spend all day making it!

PREPARATION:

Remove the eggs from the refrigerator and separate into a measuring cup 15-20 minutes before you begin the meringue. Save 3 of the yolks for the pie filling.

Use a medium-high speed of your mixer and beat the egg yolk until smooth. Add in the condensed milk, lemon juice and lemon zest. Beat until creamy. Pour mixture into prepared pie crust.

Preheat conventional or convection oven to 325°.

To make the meringue, place the egg white into the metal bowl of your hand-stand mixer or into a medium mixing bowl; do not use plastic.

Beat the eggs, at high speed, until soft peaks form; about 1 1/2 - 2 minutes;

Add cream of tartar if peaks are not forming!

Gradually add in the sugar and continue beating until meringue is thick and firmly peaks. Spread the meringue on top of the filled piecrust; be sure to go all the way to the edges.

Bake pie 12-15 minutes or until meringue is golden brown. Cool completely on a wire rack before serving.

Sour Cream Lemon Cake

This is a good dessert when you want a little something that is not too heavy. This is also a good brunch, lunch or picnic cake.

PREPARATION:

Preheat oven to 350°. Lightly grease a bundt pan with Crisco, making sure to get into any grooves.

To make the cake batter, sift the flour, baking powder, baking soda and salt together and set aside.

In a separate large mixing bowl, use your hand mixer and beat together the sugar and butter until light and fluffy. Add the lemon juice and zest and then beat in the eggs, one at a time, until mixture is thoroughly blended.

Add half of the dry mixture and half of the sour cream to the egg mixture and blend well. Add the remaining dry mixture and sour cream and beat mixture until the batter is creamy.

Pour the batter into the prepared bundt pan and bake for 40-45 minutes or until toothpick cokes out clean. Cool on a wire rack for 10 minutes and then invert the bundt cake onto a platter to cool completely.

Prepare the glaze by stirring the lemon juice into the Confectioner's sugar until smooth. Pour glaze over cooled cake and serve.

INGREDIENTS

2 1/2 cups all purpose flour

1 teaspoon baking powder

1 teaspoon baking soda

1 teaspoon salt

1 1/2 cup sugar

1 stick unsalted butter

4 eggs

1 cup sour cream

2 teaspoons grated lemon zest

2 teaspoons lemon juice

Glaze:

2/3 cup confectioners sugar; sifted

2 Tablespoons lemon juice

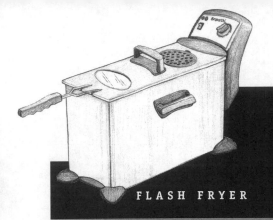

FLASH FRYER

Funnel Cakes–like you get at the Fair!

INGREDIENTS

2 eggs lightly beaten

1 1/2 cups milk

1/4 cup brown sugar firmly packed

2 cups all-purpose flour

1 1/2 teaspoons baking powder

1/4 teaspoon salt

Confectioner's sugar

These are terrific! They taste best if you use your flash fryer to cook them.

PREPARATION:

Preheat your fryer to 375°.

To make the batter, combine the eggs, milk and brown sugar in a bowl. Sift together the flour, baking powder and salt and add to the egg mixture. Beat the ingredients together until thoroughly mixed.

Traditionally, you would hold your thumb over the end of a funnel and pour in 1/2 cup batter. Then, while holding the funnel over the hot oil, you would release your thumb and drizzle the batter into the oil in a swirling motion.

I use a cleaned squeeze bottle (like ketchup) for my batter, instead of a funnel. I think it's easier to control.

Either way, once the batter is in the oil, let it fry about two minutes, turn it over and cook another two minutes until the cake is golden brown on both sides.

Drain briefly on a clean paper towel. Liberally sprinkle one side with Confectioner's sugar and serve hot.

Ice Cream–in your Food Processor!

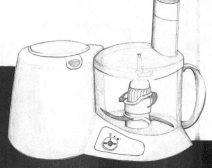

This is perhaps my most requested recipe! I make this ice cream using the Quad-Blade Processor on HSN and everyone is "wowed" because it is so easy. Try it for yourself and see if it doesn't taste as good as it looks!

FOR STRAWBERRY:

Place the frozen berries evenly around the quad-blades of your processor. Add the sugar and half and half.

Pulse the machine 3 times and then turn to highest speed until creamy. Remove the lid and push down any berries that have not been thoroughly chopped and process another few seconds if needed.

FOR BLUEBERRY, BLACKBERRY, RASPBERRY OR PEACH:

Place the frozen fruit evenly around the quad-blades of your processor. Add the sugar. Pulse the machine 3 times.

Turn to lowest speed and slowly pour the half and half down the food shoot until the mixture becomes creamy. Depending on the size of the berries or peaches, you may only need 3/4 cup half and half or you may need the entire cup!

Remove the lid and push down any berries that have not been thoroughly chopped and process another few seconds if needed.

SUGAR-FREE FAT-FREE VARIATION:

Use Splenda or Equal instead of the sugar and Fat-Free Half and Half!

Traditional Custard-Style Vanilla Ice Creams

Making real, custard-style ice cream may take a little effort and planning, but it is well worth it. The mixture will keep in your refrigerator for 2- 3 weeks so you can make it when you have the time and be ready for ice cream on demand!

I have three versions of vanilla ice cream for you to try; traditional, light and lightest! Try them all see which your family's favorite is!

Each recipe makes about 1 quart, so increase the recipe according to the size of your ice cream maker or your make-ahead desire.

INGREDIENTS

Strawberry Ice Cream:

1 16-ounce bag frozen whole strawberries

1/2 cup sugar

1 cup half and half

Blueberry, Blackberry, Raspberry or Peach Ice Cream:

1 16-ounce bag frozen whole berries or peaches

1/2 cup sugar

3/4 - 1 cup half and half

Traditional Vanilla Bean Ice Cream

INGREDIENTS

1 3/4 cups half and half

3/4 cup whipping cream

1 Tablespoon vanilla bean paste or
1 vanilla bean split lengthwise

1/2 cup sugar

5 large egg yolks

1/4 cup light corn syrup

PREPARATION:

In a medium mixing bowl, whisk together the sugar, egg yolks and corn syrup.

Combine, in a heavy medium saucepan over low heat, the half-and-half, cream and the vanilla paste or the seeds scraped from the bean. Bring this mixture just to a simmer, stirring often. When it reaches a light simmer, gradually stir it into the yolk mixture. Return the mixture to the saucepan.

Use a rubber or wooden spatula and stir the mixture, over medium-low heat, until the mixture coats the spatula. This takes about 10 minutes. Do not let the mixture come to a boil!

Transfer mixture to a bowl or pitcher, cover and refrigerate until cold.

Process ice cream mixture according to the directions with your ice cream maker.

Light Vanilla Ice Cream

INGREDIENTS

1 1/2 cup whole milk

1 1/2 cup heavy cream

3 egg yolks

1/4 cup sugar

2 teaspoons vanilla extract or seeds from 1 vanilla bean

PREPARATION:

In a medium mixing bowl, whisk together the sugar, egg yolks and vanilla.

Combine, in a heavy medium saucepan over low heat, the milk and cream. Bring this mixture just to a simmer, stirring often. When it reaches a light simmer, gradually stir it into the yolk mixture. Return the mixture to the saucepan.

Use a rubber or wooden spatula and stir the mixture, over medium-low heat, about 5-7 minutes or until it begins to thicken. Do not let the mixture come to a boil!

Transfer mixture to a bowl or pitcher, cover and refrigerate until cold.

Process ice cream mixture according to the directions with your ice cream maker.

Lightest Vanilla Ice Cream

INGREDIENTS

1 1/2 cup 2% low fat milk

1 1/2 cup nonfat evaporated skim milk

2 egg whites or 1/2 cup egg substitute

1/4 cup sugar

2 teaspoons vanilla extract or seeds from 1 vanilla bean

PREPARATION:

In a medium mixing bowl, whisk together the sugar, egg and vanilla.

In a heavy medium saucepan over low heat, bring the milks just to a simmer, stirring often. When it reaches a light simmer, gradually stir it into the egg mixture. Return the mixture to the saucepan.

Use a rubber or wooden spatula and stir the mixture, over medium-low heat, until mixture just comes to a boil. Mixture will thicken as it cools.

Transfer mixture to a bowl or pitcher, cover and refrigerate until cold.

Process ice cream mixture according to the directions with your ice cream maker.

Chocolate Ice Cream

INGREDIENTS

Makes 1 Quart

2 ounces unsweetened chocolate

1 1/2 cups milk

3/4 cup sugar

Pinch salt

1 1/2 teaspoons vanilla extract

1 1/2 cups heavy cream

PREPARATION:

In a double boiler, over boiling water, melt the chocolate with the milk. Stir in the sugar and salt and continue cooking until sugar is completely melted. Remove from heat.

Use the whisk attachment on your hand mixer and beat on low speed until mixture is cool and fluffy.

Add the vanilla and heavy cream and beat another 2 minutes.

Process ice cream mixture according to the directions with your ice cream maker.

ROCKY ROAD VARIATION:

Follow the instructions above to make the ice cream mixture. Pour only 2 3/4 cups of the mix into your ice cream maker.

When the ice cream is almost ready, or when the ice cream maker indicates, add to the mixture:

1/2 cup chocolate chunks or chips
1/2 cup mini marshmallows
1/2 cup chopped walnuts or pecans

Allow ice cream to continue churning until done.

Peppermint Candy Ice Cream

INGREDIENTS

Makes 1 Quart

1 3/4 cups (7 ounces) striped peppermint candy discs or canes

2 cups half and half

3 large egg yolks

1 cup heavy cream

1 teaspoon vanilla extract

Sure to become a holiday favorite in your household!

PREPARATION:

In a double boiler, over simmering water, combine all but 1/2 cup of the peppermint candy with the half and half. Cook until scalded. Remove from heat and let steep 15 minutes or until the candy is completely melted.

In a small mixing bowl, beat the egg yolks. Slowly beat into the eggs 1/2 cup of the hot half and half mixture. Return this mixture to the pan and cook over simmering water, stirring constantly, until the mixture coats the spoon. Immediately place the pan into a pan of very cold water and stir to cool to room temperature.

Stir in the cream and vanilla. Cover and refrigerate until cold.

Pour the cold mixture into your ice cream maker and churn according to directions. When ice cream is almost frozen, mix in the remaining candy.

Coffee Ice Cream

This is one of my favorite ice creams to serve as a dessert at an adult dinner. I serve it atop a chocolate brownie and drizzle it with warm caramel syrup; yummy!

PREPARATION:

In a double boiler, over rapidly boiling water, scald the milk. Reduce heat and add the sugar; stir until completely dissolved.

In a small mixing bowl, beat the egg yolks. Slowly beat into the eggs 1/2 cup of the hot milk mixture. Return this mixture to the pan and cook over simmering water, stirring constantly, until the mixture coats the spoon.

Remove from heat and chill.

Stir in the coffee, salt, whipping cream and vanilla. Cover and refrigerate until cold.

Pour the cold mixture into your ice cream maker and churn according to directions.

INGREDIENTS

Makes 1 Quart

1 3/4 cups milk

1 1/4 cups sugar

2 beaten eggs

1/3 cup strong cold coffee

1/2 teaspoon salt

1 cup whipping cream

1 teaspoon vanilla

Strawberry Ice Cream

INGREDIENTS

2 cups fresh strawberries

1/2 cup sugar

1 teaspoon lemon juice

1 cup half and half

1 cup heavy cream

4 egg yolks

3 drops red food coloring (optional)

I like chunks of strawberry in my ice cream, but you may puree your berries if desired.

PREPARATION:

Wash and hull the strawberries. Place them into your food processor and pulse until chopped to desired consistency. Place the berries into a glass bowl and toss with 4 Tablespoons of the sugar and the lemon juice. Cover and refrigerate 1 hour or until the sugar has dissolved.

Combine the half and half and cream in a sauce pan and heat to almost boiling.

In a medium mixing bowl, whisk together the egg yolks and remaining sugar until light. Continue whisking while pouring the milk mixture into the eggs.

Return mixture to sauce pan and cook over low heat, stirring constantly, until mixture coats the back of a spoon. Remove from heat and let cool.

Stir in the strawberries and juice and add a couple drops of red food coloring if desired. Cover and refrigerate until thoroughly cold.

Follow the directions of your ice cream maker and freeze ice cream.

Butter Pecan Ice Cream

This is my all-time favorite ice cream!

PREPARATION:

In a medium mixing bowl, whisk together the sugar, egg yolks and corn syrup.

Combine, in a heavy medium saucepan over low heat, the half-and-half and cream. Bring this mixture just to a simmer, stirring often. When it reaches a light simmer, gradually stir it into the yolk mixture. Return the mixture to the saucepan.

Use a rubber or wooden spatula and stir the mixture, over medium-low heat, until the mixture coats the spatula. This takes about 5-7 minutes. Do not let the mixture come to a boil! Remove from heat and let cool. Add the butter flavoring.

Transfer mixture to a bowl or pitcher, cover and refrigerate until cold.

Process ice cream mixture according to the directions with your ice cream maker. When the mixture is almost completely frozen, add the pecans.

INGREDIENTS

1 3/4 cups half and half

3/4 cup whipping cream

1/2 cup sugar

5 large egg yolks

1/4 cup light corn syrup

2 teaspoons Imitation Butter Flavoring

1/2 cup coarsely chopped pecans

Orange Cream Sherbet

INGREDIENTS

1 teaspoon imitation orange flavoring or 1 1/2 teaspoons grated orange rind

1 cup sugar

1/4 cup water

1 cup no-pulp orange juice

2 cups half and half

Orange food coloring (optional)

This is my son Max's favorite ice cream!

PREPARATION:

Combine the orange flavoring (or rind) with the sugar and water in a small saucepan over medium low heat. Stir the mixture until the sugar has completely dissolved. Remove from heat and cool.

Pour this mixture into a bowl and stir in the orange juice and half and half. If the milk curdles slightly, it will not alter the taste or texture once frozen. Cover and refrigerate until cold.

Pour mixture into your ice cream maker and freeze according to the directions.

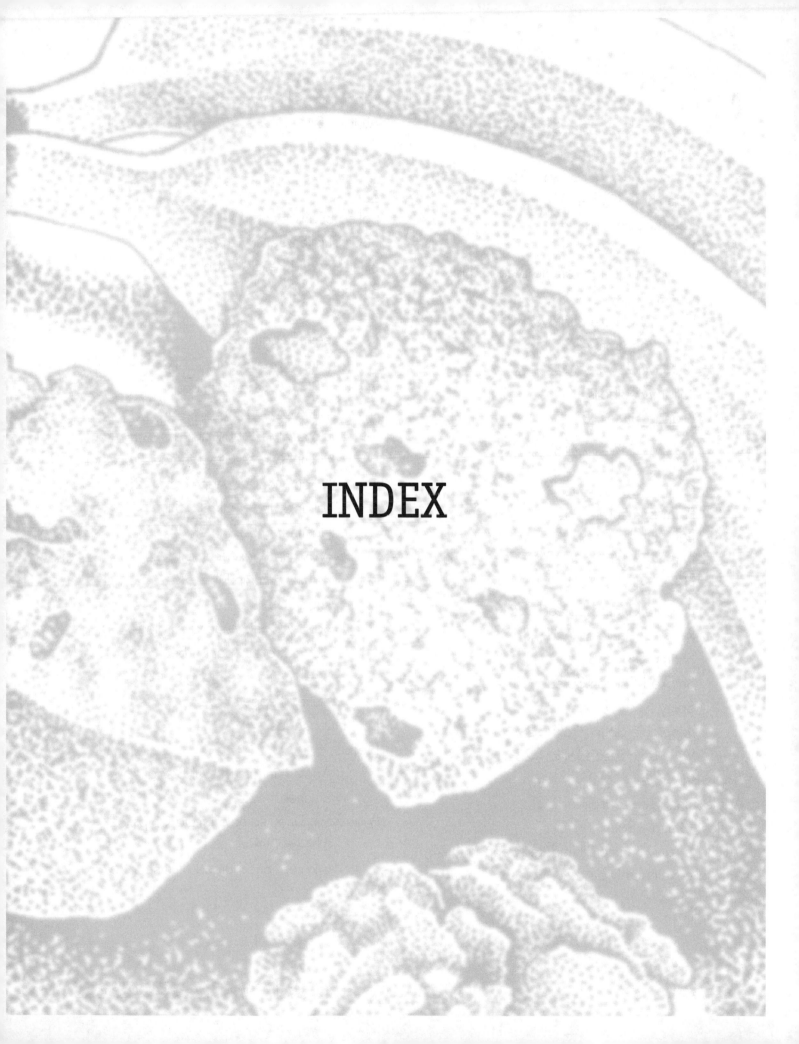

INDEX

BONUS RECIPES

Since the first printing of this book, Bravetti has added a new 8 Liter fryer to it's inventory. Because this fryer cooks 3.5 pounds of food at one time, I have added a couple of new recipes for you to try. I hope you enjoy them!

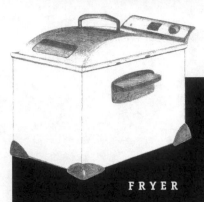

Deep Fried Turkey Breast

INGREDIENTS

Vegetable or Peanut oil for frying

1/2 bone-in turkey breast
(about 3 - 3 1/2 lbs.)

Salt and pepper

Optional:

3 cups flour

3 cups milk

This is an easy way to enjoy fried turkey without having to get out the huge propane fryer! This is a basic recipe that tastes great, but if you like a more seasoned flavor, rub with garlic salt, Cajun seasoning, seasoned salt or whatever you like, and let sit in the refrigerator overnight before frying…mmm good!

PREPARATION:

Fill the fryer to just below the maximum fill line, insert the largest basket and heat to 375°.

Wash, pat dry and season the turkey liberally with salt and pepper. If breading is desired, dredge the turkey in flour, then milk, and back in the flour. Carefully lower the breast into the hot oil and fry until golden brown and cooked to 165∞ on an instant read thermometer (about 6 minutes per pound).

Southern-Fried Corn on the Cob

INGREDIENTS

Vegetable oil for frying

Fresh corn on the cob

I thought I made this recipe up one day, but then my friend Tracy told me she had enjoyed it at a deep-south barbeque joint! Either way...it is delicious!

PREPARATION:

Fill the fryer to at least the halfway mark between the minimum and maximum fill lines, insert the largest basket and heat to 385°.

Without using water, remove the husk and silk from the corn and brush clean.

Carefully lower the corn (up to 6 ears at a time) into the oil and fry for 3 minutes. Remove from oil and drain on paper towels.

Granddaddy's Fried Fish

INGREDIENTS

4 nice white fish filets
(about 1 - 1 1/2 pounds)

Salt and pepper

1 cup flour

1 cup mashed potato flakes

1 egg

1 cup milk

My Grandfather taught me to add mashed potato flakes to my fish batter and I really like the flavor it gives the fish. Try it for yourself and see what you think!

PREPARATION:

Fill the fryer to at least the halfway mark between the minimum and maximum fill lines, insert the largest basket and heat to 385°.

Wash, pat dry and liberally season the fillets with salt and pepper.

Mix the flour and potato flakes together on a plate or in a shallow bowl.

Beat the egg with the milk in a shallow bowl.

Dip the fish first into the milk mixture and then press into the flour mixture to completely coat the fillet. Repeat with the remaining fillets.

Carefully place the fillets into the lowered basket in the hot oil. Fry until golden brown; 4 - 6 minutes depending on the thickness of the fillets.

Homemade Cake Donuts

These aren't as hard as they seem, they just take a little while to make!

PREPARATION:

In a large bowl, beat the eggs & sugar together with your hand mixer until thick. Add the sour cream, butter and vanilla and mix until well combined. In a separate bowl, sift together the flour, baking powder and salt. Using your dough hooks, mix the dry mixture into the wet, one cup at a time, until the dough is sticky and begins to pull away from the sides.

Generously flour a large working surface and place the dough on it. Dust the dough with more flour and roll or pat it out until it is about 1/3-inch thick. Let the dough sit for 15 minutes. Use a donut cutter or a 2 1/2-inch round for the outside and a 1-inch round for the center and cut the dough into donut shapes. Try to cut the donuts close together to yield as many donuts as possible, because rolling the dough again will make it tough.

Fit the fryer with the largest basket. Fill the fryer with enough oil so that it has at least 3 inches above the bottom of the basket and heat to 365°.

Fry the doughnuts, 6 at a time, for 1-2 minutes on each side, or until they are golden brown. Remove and drain on paper towels. Fry the doughnut holes, 8-10 at a time, for 45 seconds on each side, or until they are golden brown, and drain them on paper towels.

While the donuts are still warm, cover with chocolate, glaze, powdered sugar or cinnamon sugar and enjoy!

INGREDIENTS

2 large eggs

2/3 cup sugar

2/3 cup sour cream

3 Tablespoons butter; melted and cooled

2 cups flour

1 teaspoon vanilla

2 teaspoons double acting baking powder

1 teaspoon baking soda

1/2 teaspoon salt

Vegetable oil for frying